I am full of energy and joy.

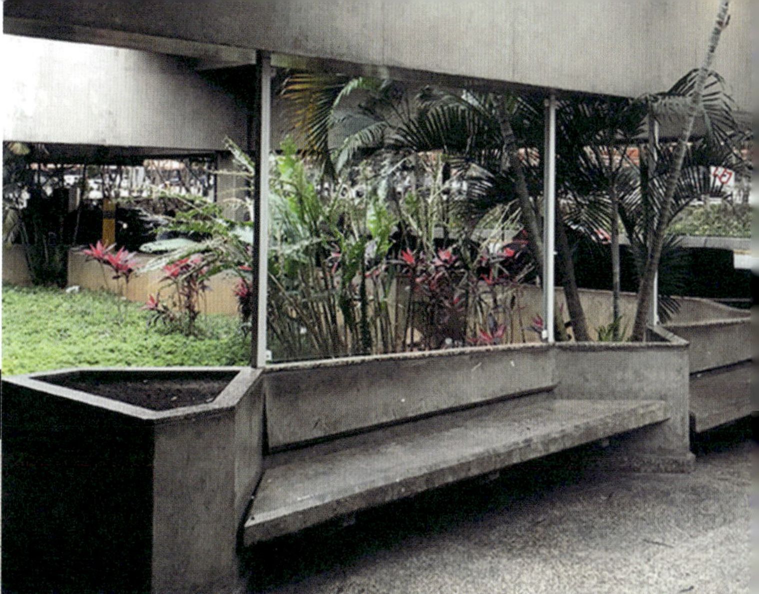

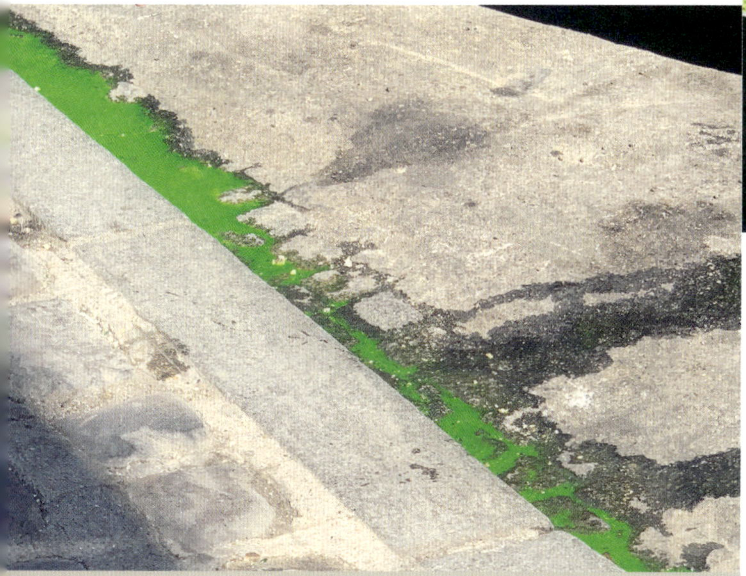

I have been blessed with endless talent that I start using today, no matter whether society invites me to be self-reliant or to believe in myself.

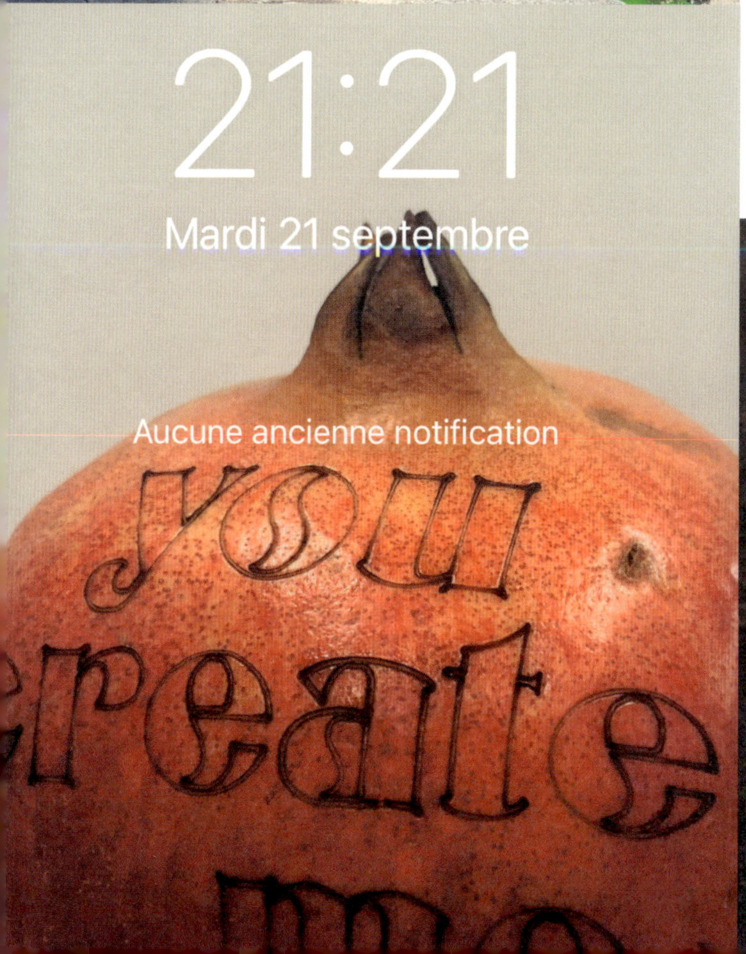

21:21
Mardi 21 septembre
Aucune ancienne notification
you
create

Temple Of Love MANIFESTO

Temple of love is an inclusive ecosystem around the notion of///love.

It appeared essential to put forward the concept of+love' as a new political fact et and to make it predominant in a

999 heterosexist, racist, homophobic, transphobic society dominated by an authoritarian and predominantly white patriarchy. ooo This' inverted and radical communitarianism must be challenged quickly by the cultural and ruling institutions..

The « Temple of love » projet began in 2 018- 201 9 at Bétonsalon, in Paris, as a preface to a geographically indeterminate cycle.

It takes shape as an uninterrupted, multidisciplinary, systemic space.

The temple must be considered as a sacred space i.e connecting the spaces of humans and 1111 Gods and spiritual entities.1111

This implies a questioning of our way of thinking about the world, the universe, the Nature that surrounds us.

I'''s of public 888 utility.

It contains its own rules and customs.))))))

m

It allows the questioning of the museum space as an entity coming from the colonial heritage.The temple of love is ecofeminist by embodying a queer « empowerment » thus inclusive..6//&

T.O.L is a space of resistance. ; ;;; and vulnerability It s'activated through meeting and sharing 9 97

oooooooo Temple of love is defined through its modes of 'apparition and its genesis according to its invitations, its location.

It s adaptable.@

The unpublished essay on l```ove by Roland Barthes,555

GAËLLE CHOISNE

Temple of Love – To Hide

KÜNSTLERHAUS BETHANIEN 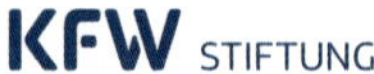

Preface

As part of the KfW Stiftung's international Artist-in-Residence programme in cooperation with Künstlerhaus Bethanien, outstanding artists are invited to live and work in Berlin for one year. The programme serves to promote talented emerging artists and at the same time acts as an incubator for new ideas, creative processes and contemporary forms of expression.

During the residency in 2020–21 the French-Haitian artist Gaëlle Choisne developed the project *To Hide*. It was created as an iteration of the artist's long-term project, *Temple of Love*. Loosely inspired by the chapter 'To Hide' from Roland Barthes' *A Lover's Discourse: Fragments* (1977), Choisne draws on concepts of healing and caring with a strong spiritual connection to nature. This includes creole traditions, myths and the cultural practices of indigenous groups. All this converges into an extensive accumulation of films, sculptures and installations that is characteristic of her work. At the same time, the center piece of *To Hide* is large hand-woven carpet – a space for spirituality and communication. In essence, Choisne creates performative spaces within the exhibition in which she encourages artistic collaboration as well as visitor participation to engage with her concept of love.

Elements of this multi-layered approach are expressed in this publication. It presents the ecosystem of *Temple of Love* and was developed in close collaboration with the artist. The distinctive, associative visual language is directly related to Choisne's work. In the accompanying essay, Wong Binghao then unfolds the practice of *Temple of Love*, expands its sensual dimensions and places it within a curatorial and discursive context.

Gaëlle Choisne's artistic approaches come together in this publication: It is a manifesto for love.

Daniela Leykam and Christoph Tannert
Editors

Contents

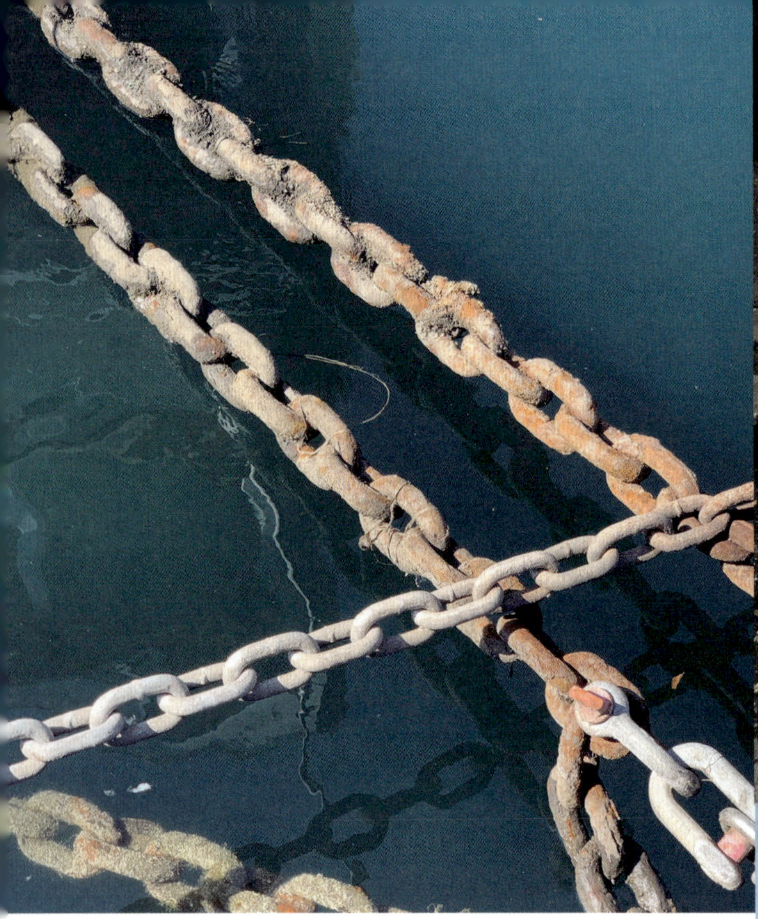

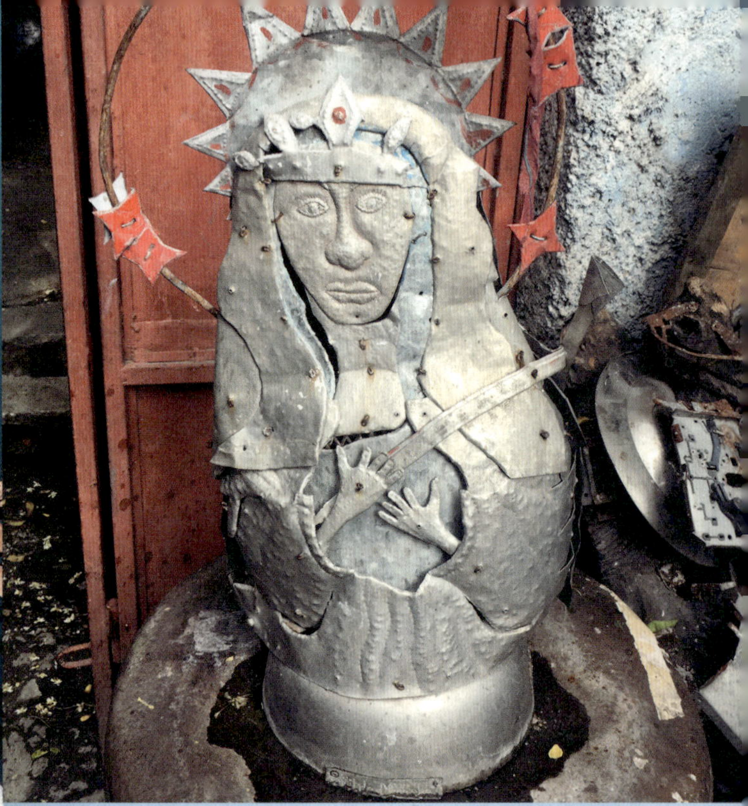

I am not afraid to face
our illusory reality: this world
is colonial.

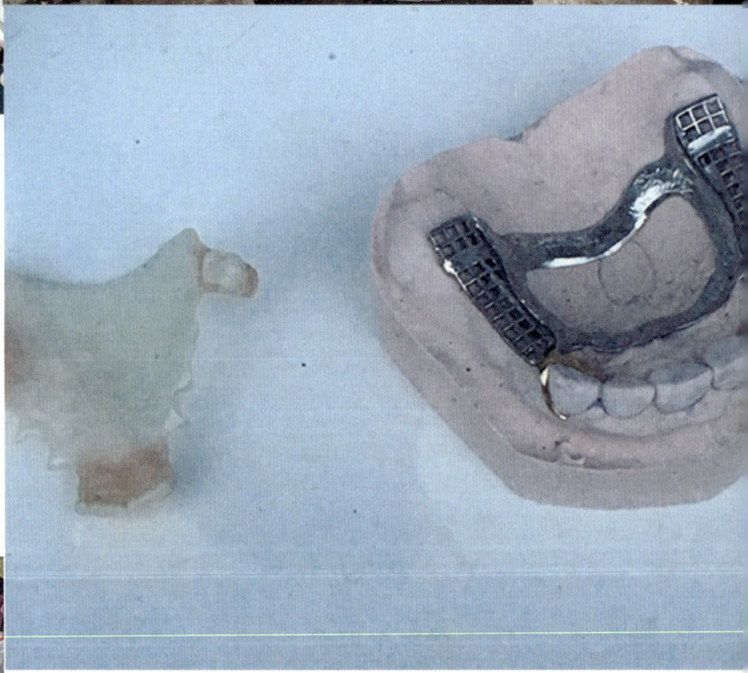

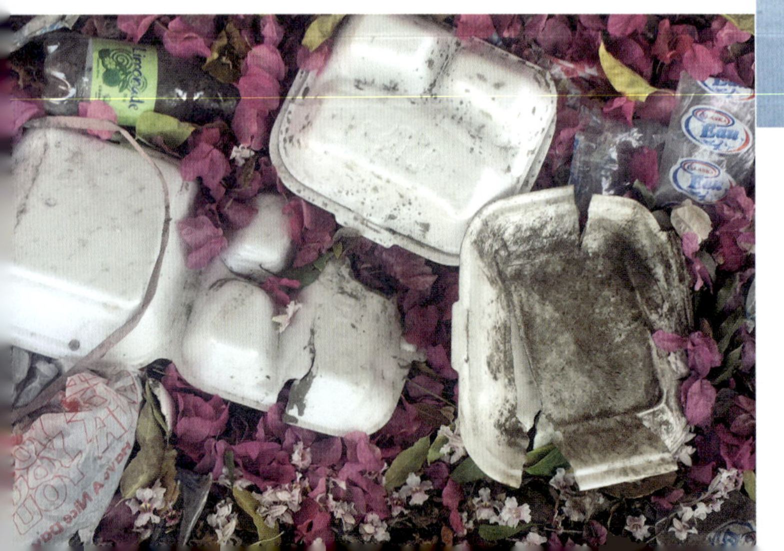

I am the architect of my own
life: I step away from brutalism.

fragments d'un discours amoureux, from 1977 will guide us through each new chapter § of Temple of love.
I»ll adapt each chapter of the,,essay from the private to the public sphere.

T.O.L is a tribute. to the invisibilized bodies, 222 to the minority and fragile souls and to ¨the dispossessed hearts..

I'act as an'artiste /and collaboration with the curators to create a set of 'Russian dolls invitations.---

888 I propose// existing works in the corpus of this project, new works produced for the new chapter,,, sometimes a new video that refers to it..

The works 444 correspond to functional sculptures acting at ££££ the crossroads of design , &¨

++art and architecture.

The functional aspect of the sculptures refers to a

TTT* desacralization of the›››art by the possibility of touching and to use those.

What I like to highlight in the project -when^ possible- are the punctual invitations --999

or permanent invitations within the exhibition, of living or dead artists to whom I pay homage, who'inspire me and whom I love ---

.: they are my « Luvs* ».

)) Luvs ; non-standard spelling of love`/6

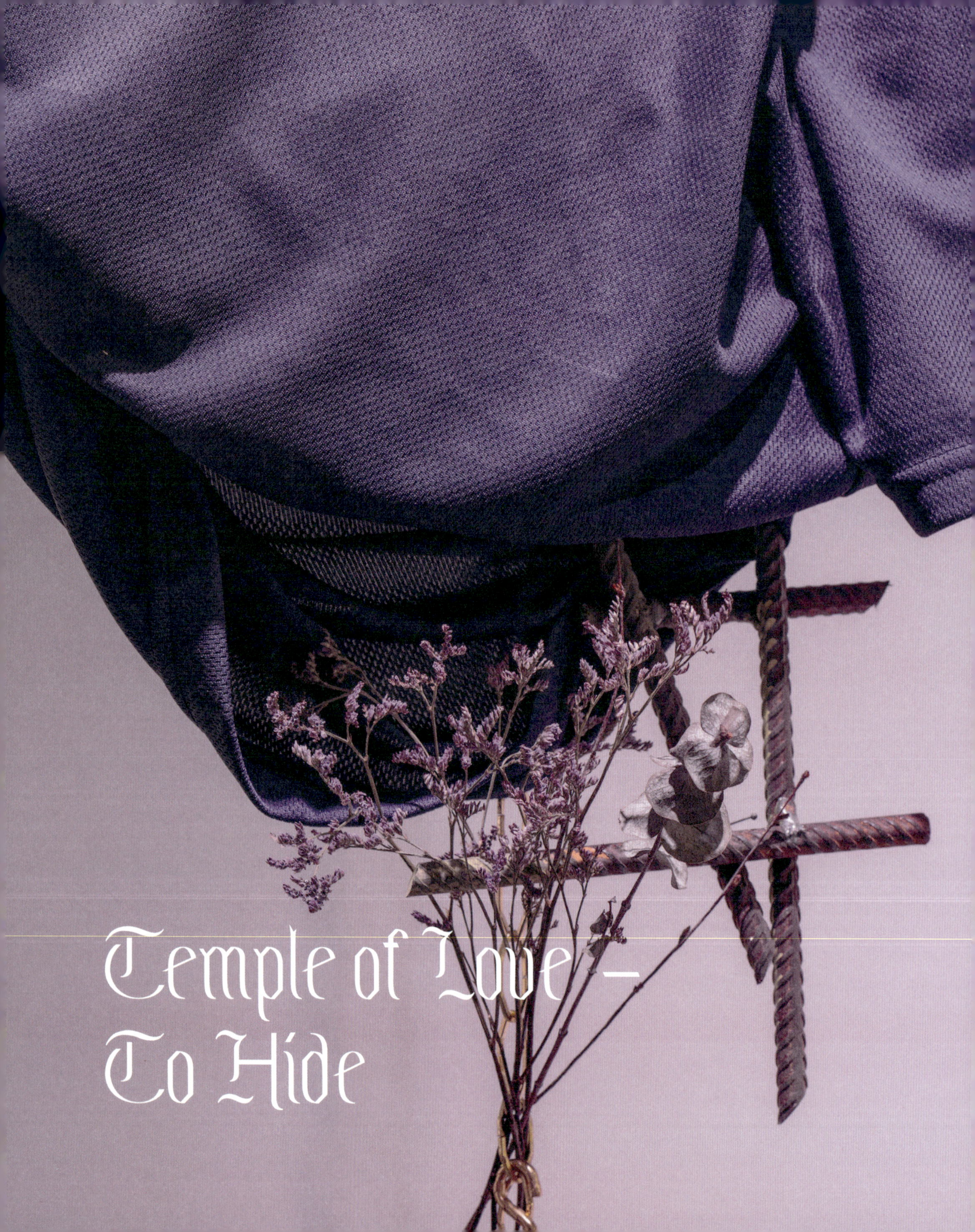

Temple of Love – To Hide

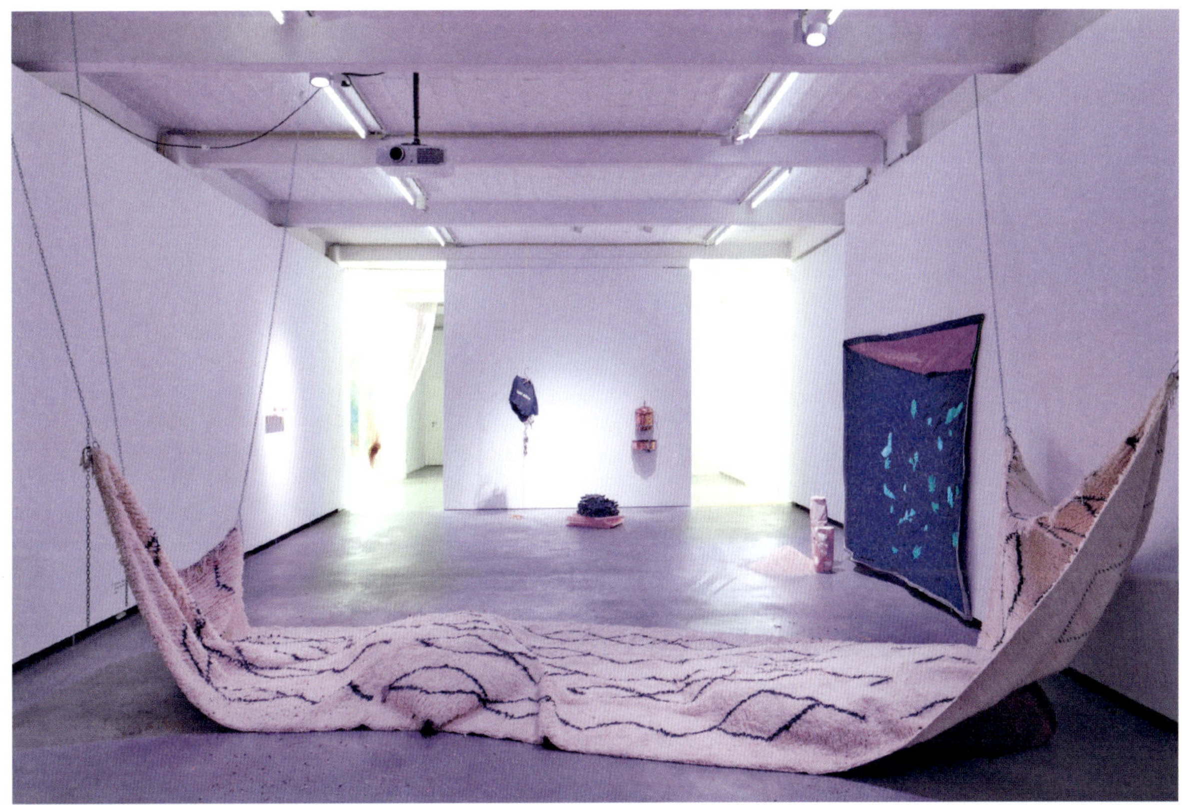

Temple of Love – To Hide, 2022, exhibition view
Left: *Paul Gilroy my bro* (detail), 2022

Temple of Love – To Hide at Künstlerhaus Bethanien, is a new phase of *Temple of Love* – a long-term project aiming at a global reunification of the living through the concept of love. This exhibition, freely inspired by the chapter 'To Hide' in Roland Barthes' *A Lover's Discourse: Fragments*, is resolutely oriented towards self-reconstruction through the sharing of experience, connection to one's ancestors, respect for heritage and inner corporal harmony.

With contributions by Ahuehuete, Pablo Altar, Arghtee, ASMR STACY, Association Agonessan, Mykki Blanco, Marie-Carmel Brouard, Cardi B, Jean Chesnel, Crystallmess, Virginie Despentes, Sidney Drew, Léo Dupré, Silvia Federici, Nadia Yala Kisukidi, Zoe Leonard, Audre Lorde, Agnes Noel, Euvonie Reynald and Megg Rayara Gomes de Oliveira, Madame Café, Karl Marx, Nicki Minaj, Djibril Sall, Spice, Lorenzo Targhetta, Christiane Taubira, Simone Thiébaut, Assa Traoré, Françoise Vergès, Amber Wagner, Tierra Whack.

My Body is a Stubborn Child

Gaëlle Choisne

In order to suggest, delicately, that I am suffering, in order to hide without lying, I shall make use of a cunning preterition: I shall divide the economy of my signs. The task of the verbal signs will be to silence, to mask, to deceive: I shall never account, verbally, *for the excesses of my sentiment. Having said nothing of the ravages of this anxiety, I can always, once it has passed, reassure myself that no one has guessed anything. The power of language: with my language I can do everything: even and especially* say nothing.

I can do everything with my language, but not with my body. *What I hide by my language, my body utters. I can deliberately mold my message, not my voice. By my voice, whatever it says, the other will recognise 'that something is wrong with me'. I am a liar (by preterition), not an actor. My body is a stubborn child, my language is a very civilised adult.*

Roland Barthes

My body is a stubborn child. The conditions of my body in its child-like state are the prerequisites of my installation *Temple of Love – To Hide*. The rug as an exhibition device recalls that joyous childhood moment of lying on the rug while watching TV. It goes even further as it reminds us that we can rely on our ancestors and lie down with a peaceful mind. The same goes for the video *Ahuehuete 1111*. Admiring nature and being able to communicate with it, being able to speak to and understand the trees – these are the messages of my exhibition.

The signs are many. So are the sinuous passages. The suspended plates betray some aspects of these sinuosities and asperities as an emotional cartography visible to all.

The language of a very civilised adult hides this bitterness. These voices, these transfeminine and feminine words embrace the 'something is wrong with me' but my question is: in relation to what and according to which system of reference?

Become a liar in this society that does not accept us as we are. The films in *Temple of Love – To Hide* denounce this invisibility, and even reveal the existence of these pockets of resistance acting in parallel with the growing primitive accumulation of capital.

I can do anything with my language but not with my body. Bodies don't lie. My black female body cannot say anything except what it is. My language can submit or say the opposite, but today it says what it is – aligned.

Dark Glasses

cacher / to hide

A deliberative figure: the amorous subject wonders, not whether he should declare his love to the loved being (this is not a figure of avowal), but to what degree he should conceal the turbulences of his passion: his desires, his distresses; in short, his excesses (in Racinian language: his *fureur*).

1. X, who left for his vacation without me, has shown no signs of life since his departure: accident? post-office strike? indifference? distancing maneuver? exercise of a passing impulse of autonomy ("His youth deafens him, he fails to hear")? or simple innocence? I grow increasingly anxious, pass through each act of the waiting-scenario. But when X reappears in one way or another, for he cannot fail to do so (a thought which should immediately dispel any anxiety), what will I say to him? Should I hide my distress—which will be over by then (*"How are you?"*)? Release it aggressively (*"That wasn't at all nice, at least you could have . . ."*) or passionately (*"Do you know how much worry you caused me?"*)? Or let this distress of mine be delicately, discreetly understood, so that it will be discovered without having to strike down the other (*"I was rather concerned . . ."*)? A secondary anxiety seizes me, which is that I must determine the degree of publicity I shall give to my initial anxiety.

Mme de Sévigné

2. I am caught up in a double discourse, from which I cannot escape. On the one hand, I tell myself: suppose

Extract from the essay *A Lover's Discourse: Fragments* (1977) by Roland Barthes

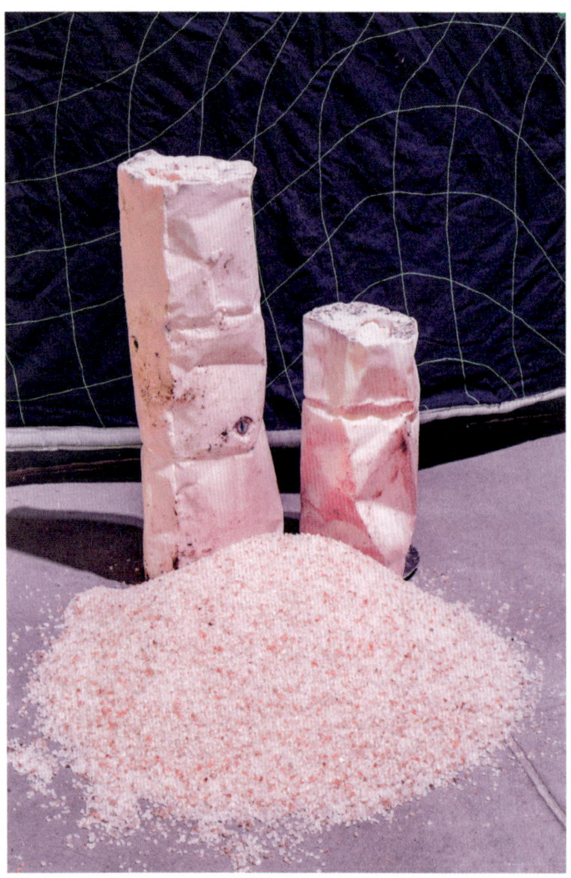

My devotion for you (detail), 2022

Paul Gilroy my bro, 2022

Page 15: *Purple water-wishes and more foreva1111illimited love.)period.*, 2022
Page 16: *L'éveil du cosmos* (detail), 2022
Page 17: *Survival kit for straight ppl*, 2022

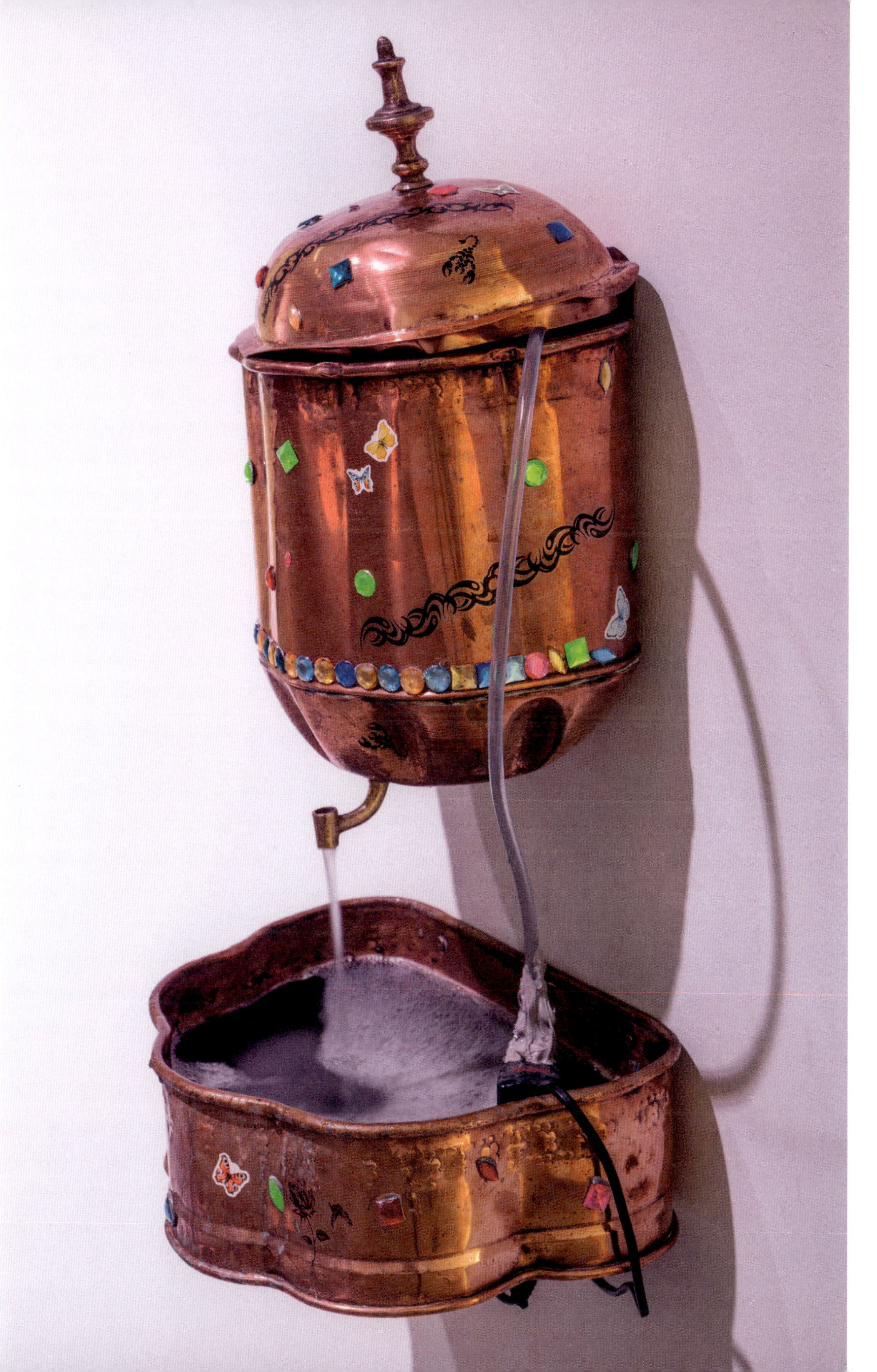

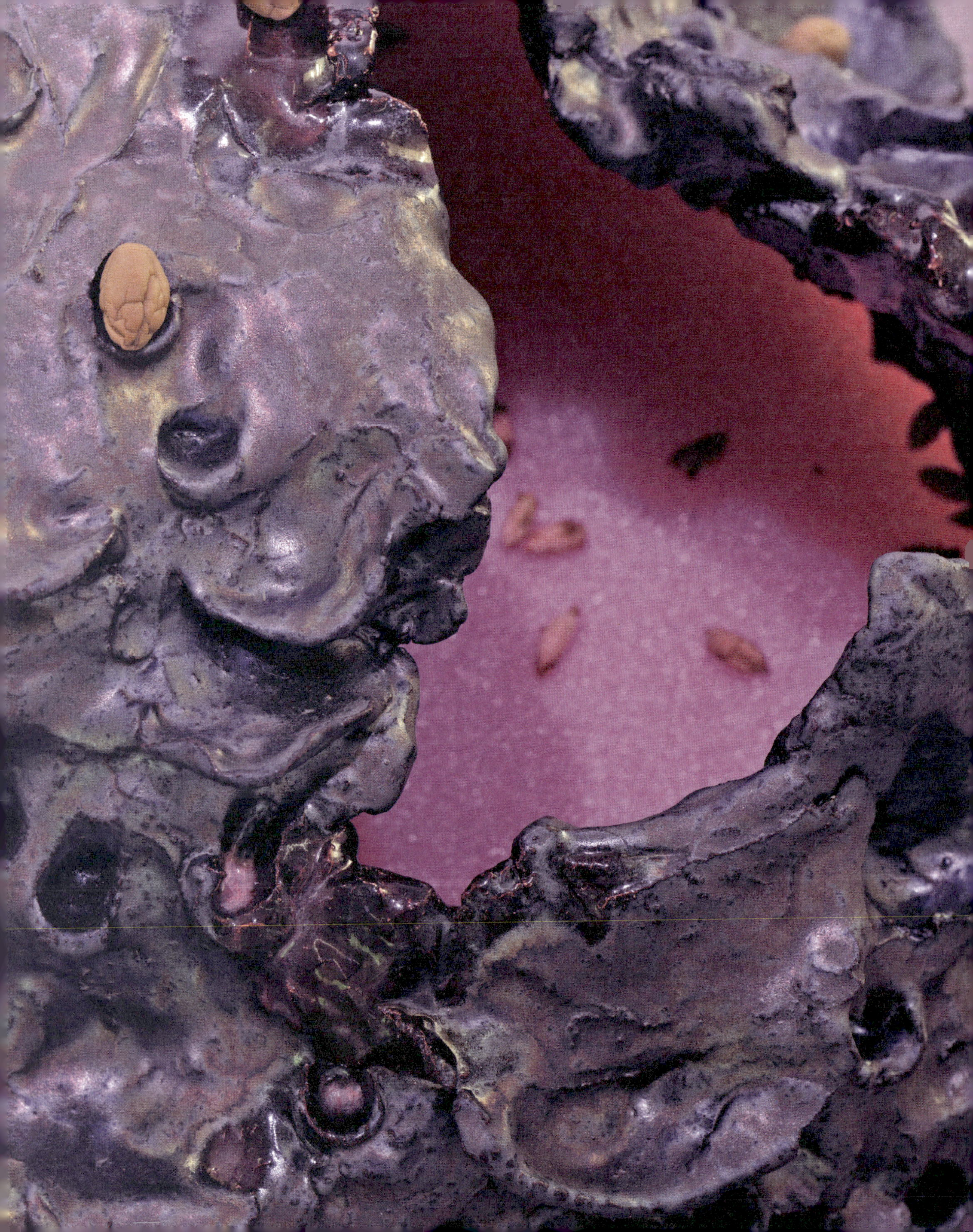

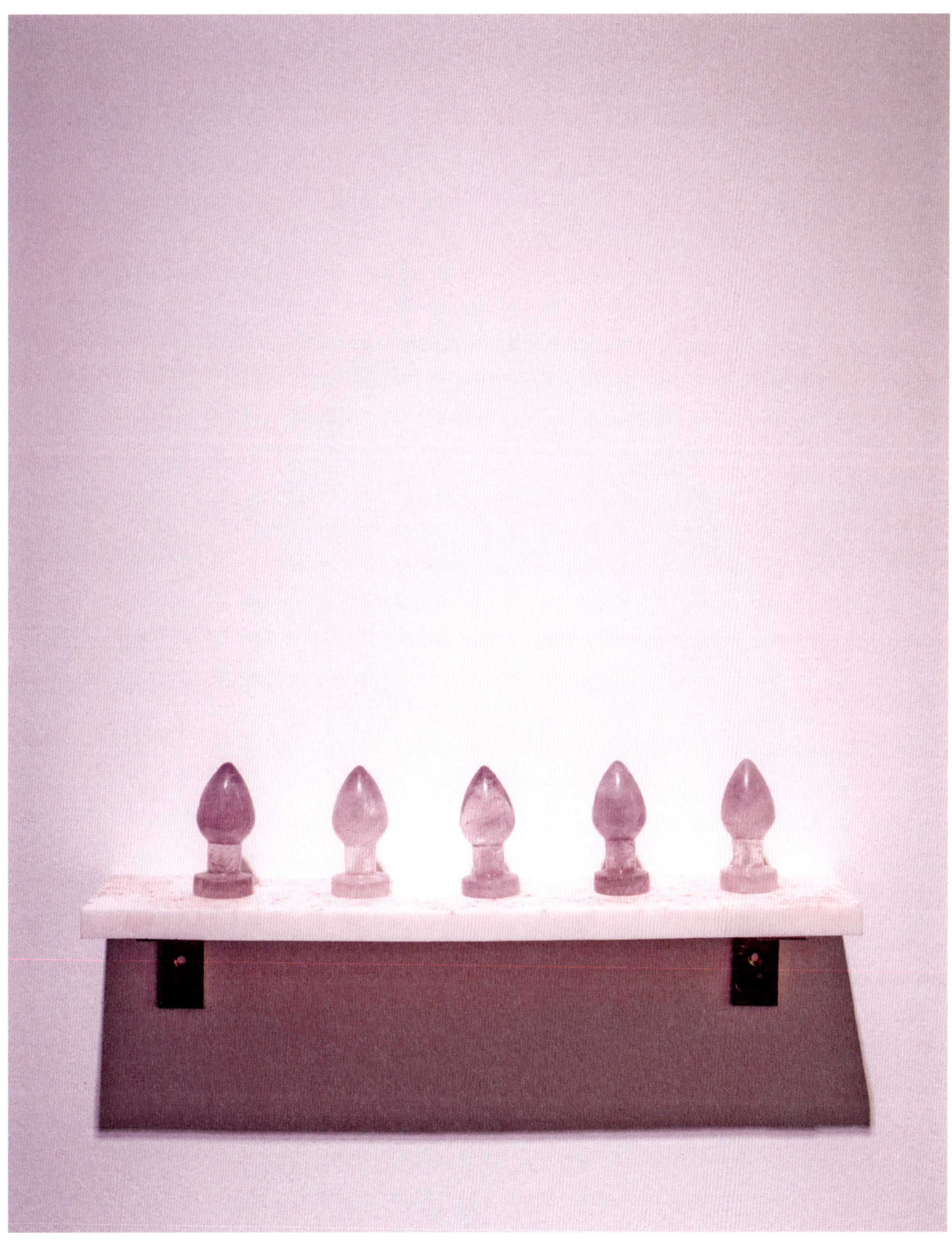

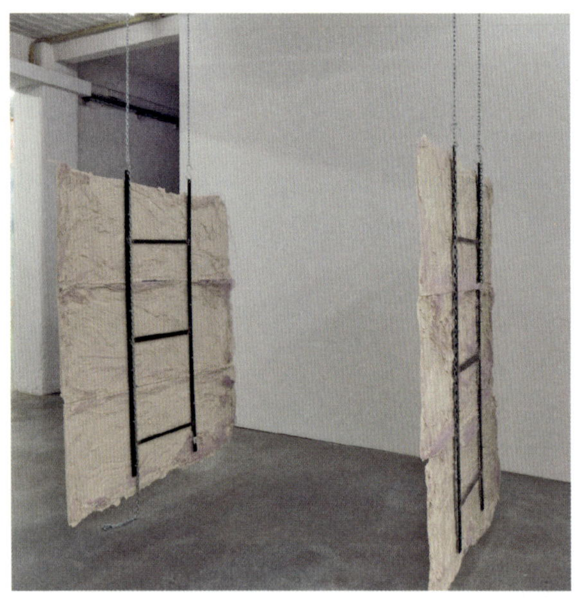
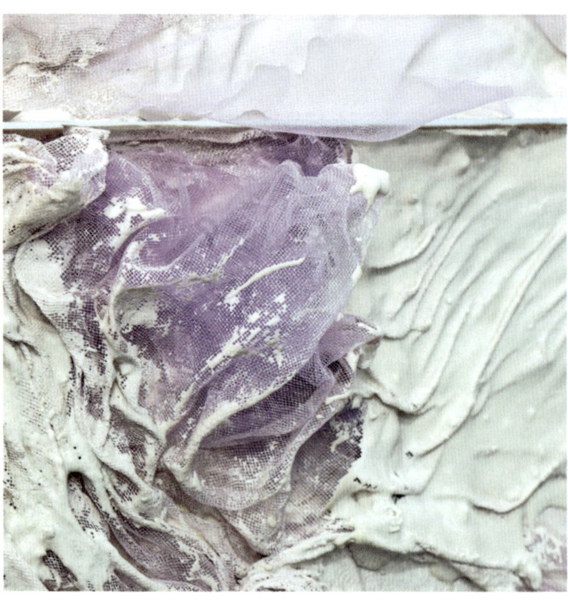
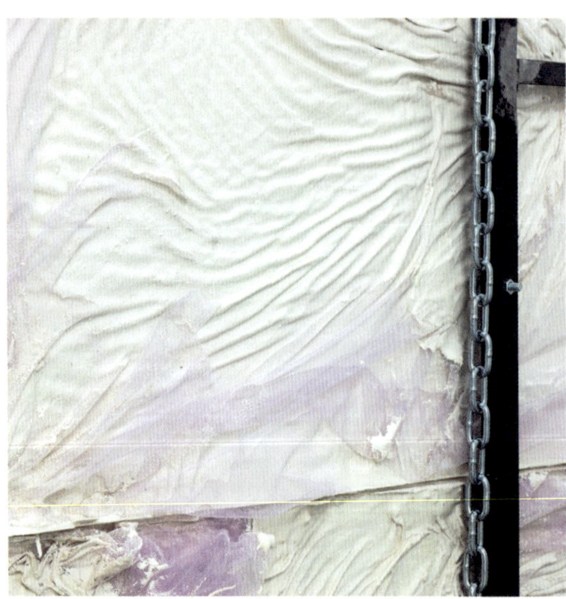
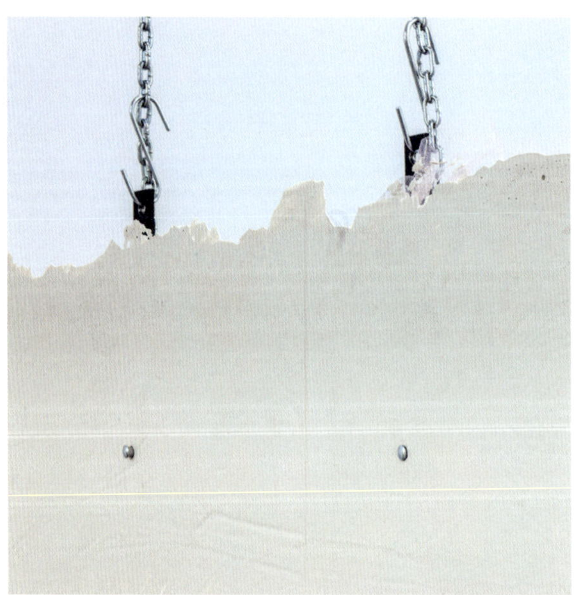

Forget the appearances 5D, 2022

Page 19: *Ahuehuete 1111*, 2022, exhibition view

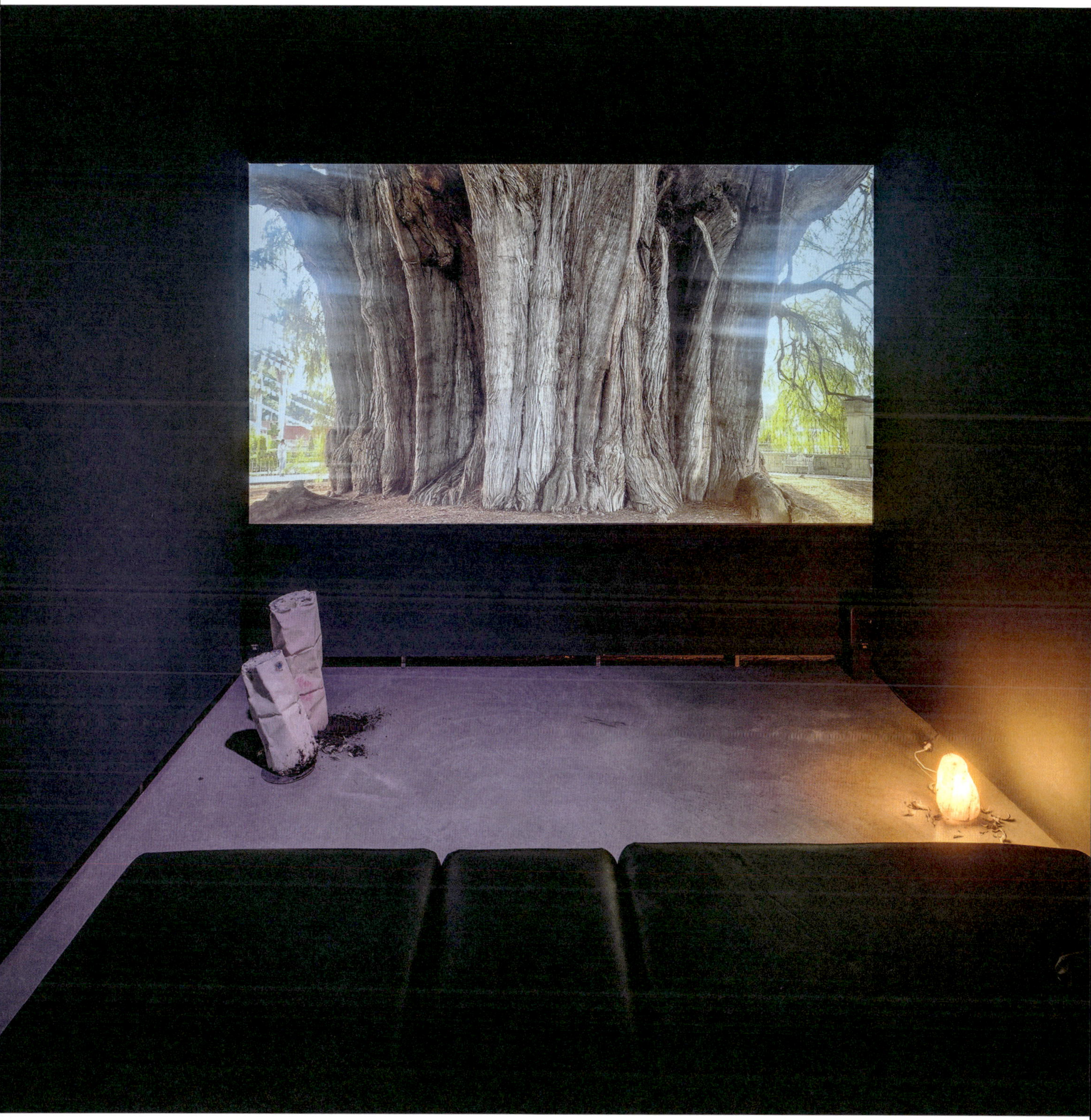

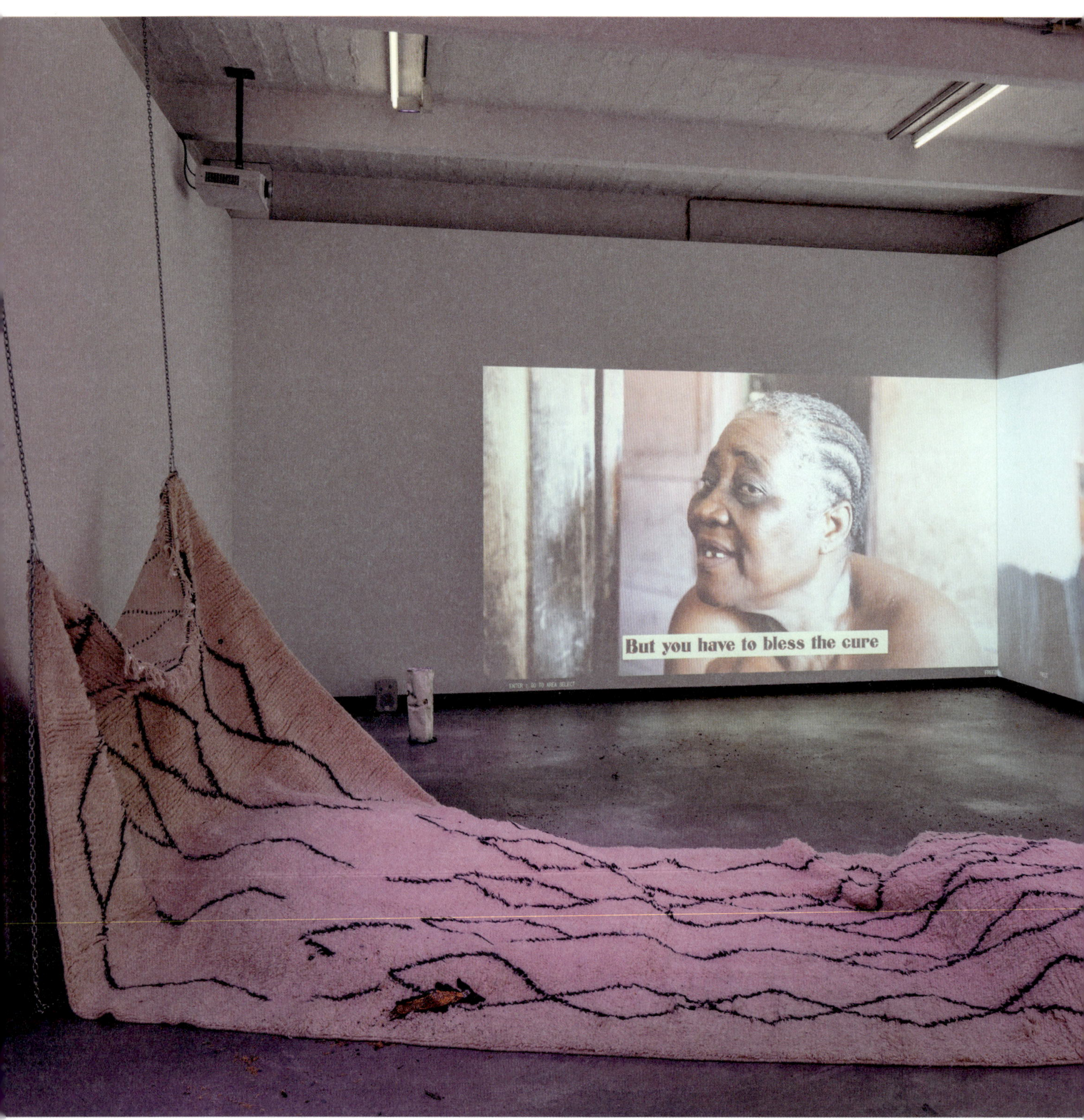
But you have to bless the cure

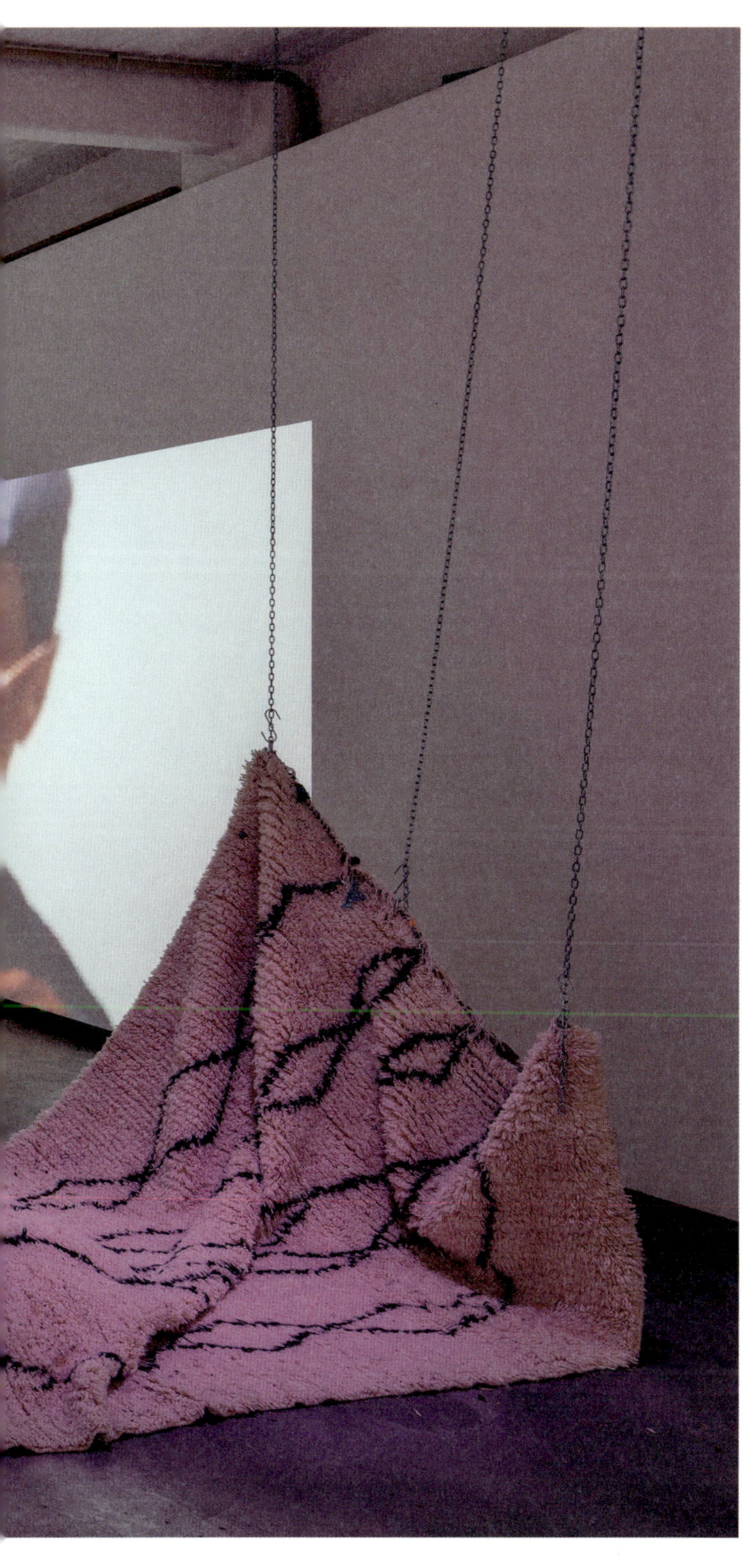

Temple of Love – To Hide, 2022, exhibition view

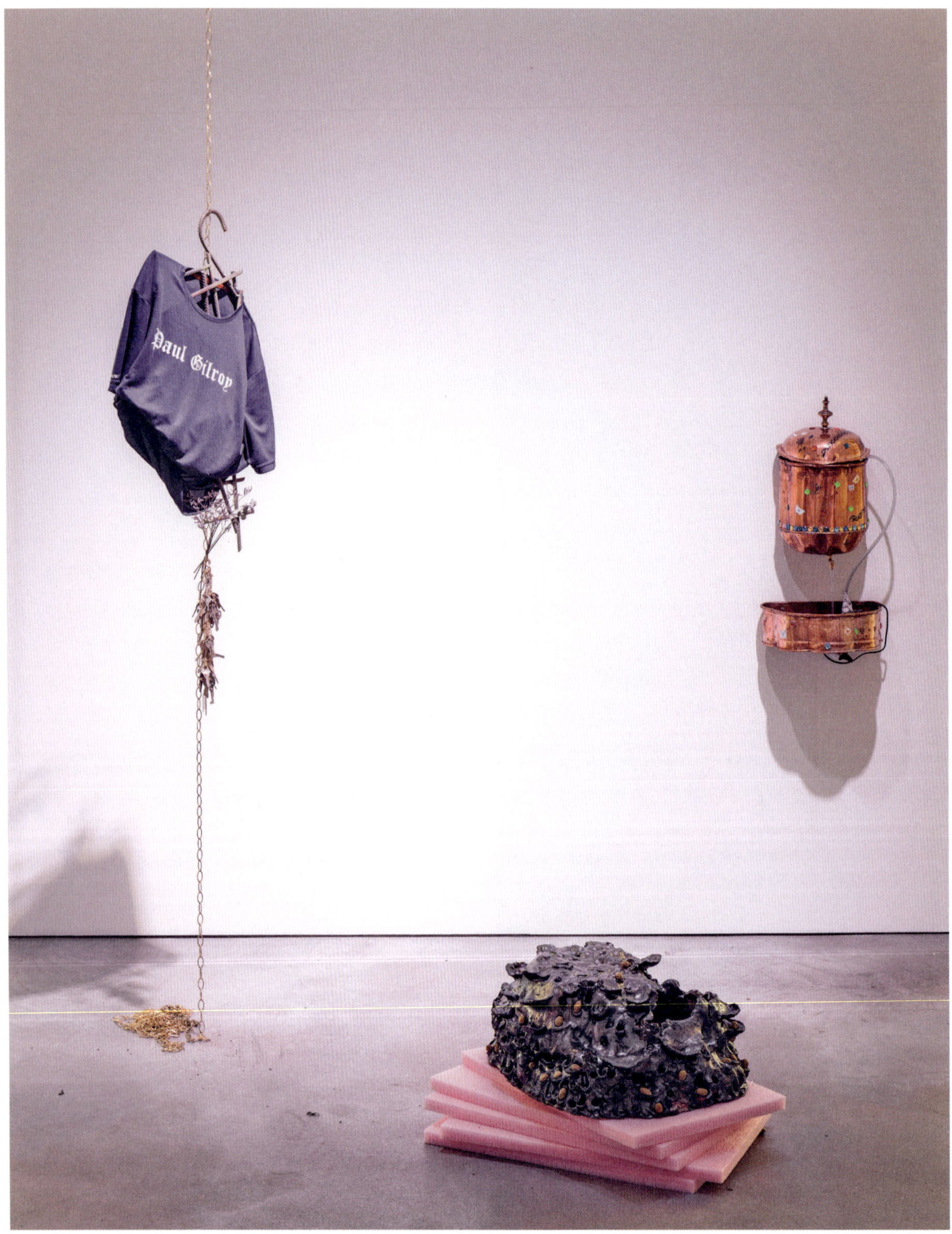
Paul Gilroy

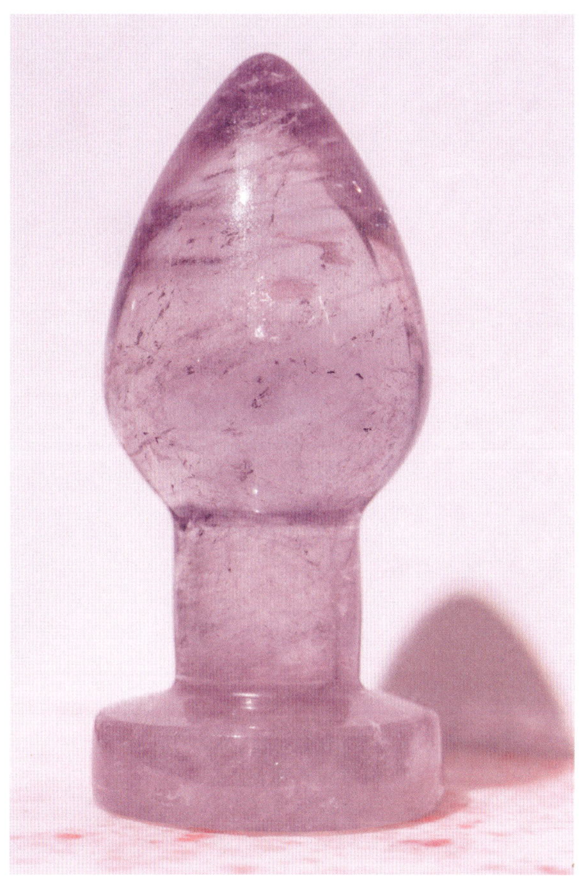

Temple of Love – To Hide, 2022, exhibition view

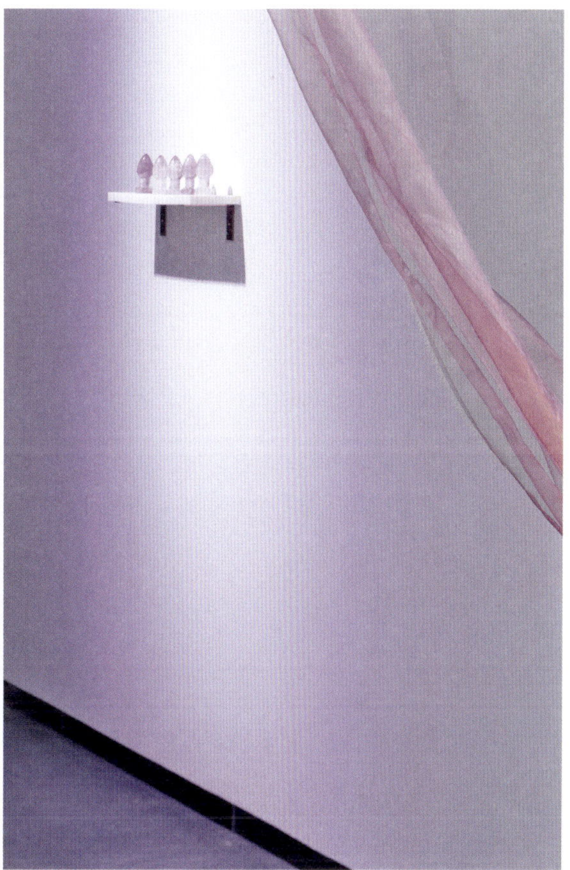

Survival kit for straight ppl, 2022

Page 22, 24: *Temple of Love – To Hide*, 2022, exhibition view

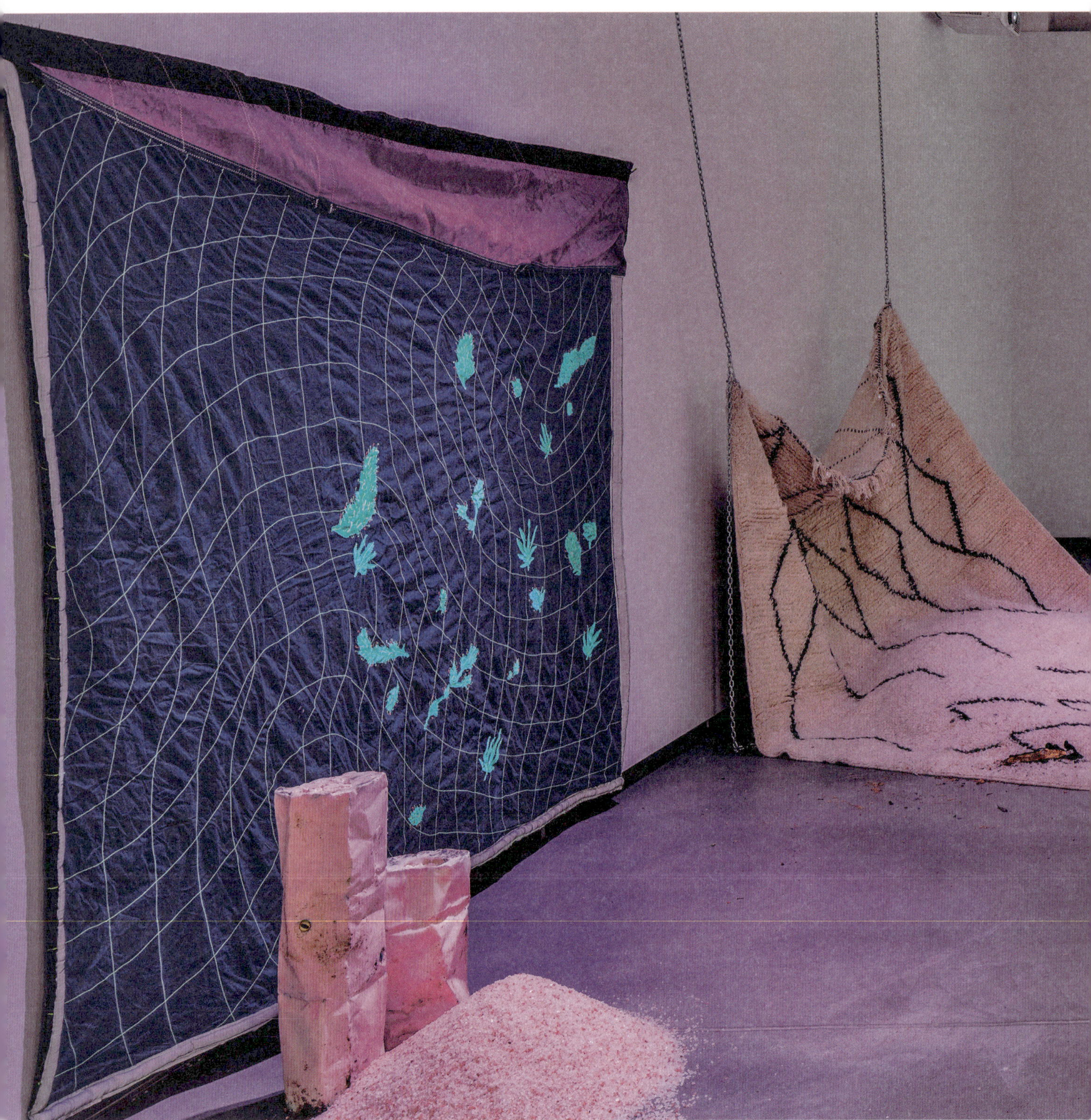

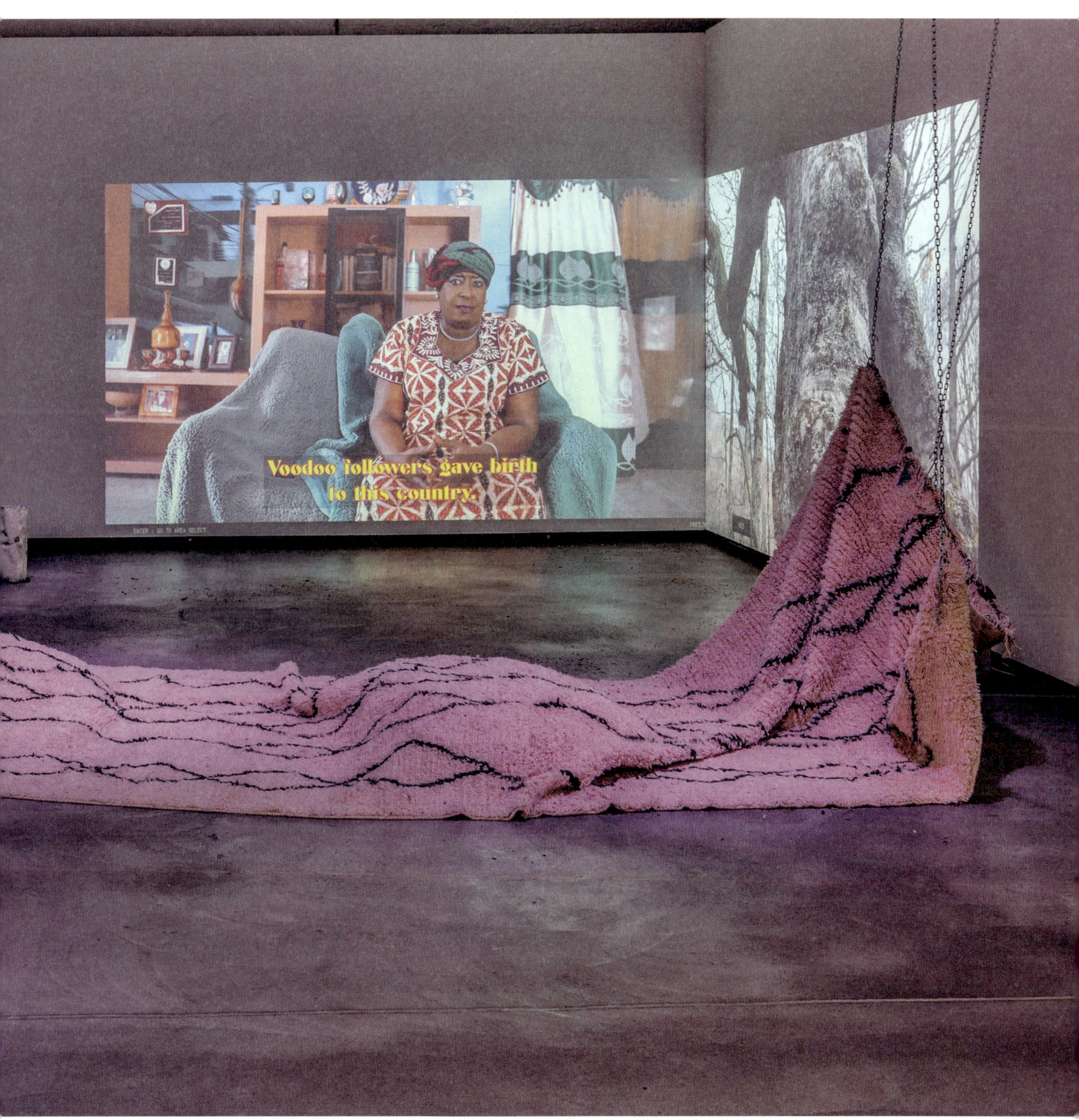
Voodoo followers gave birth
to this country.

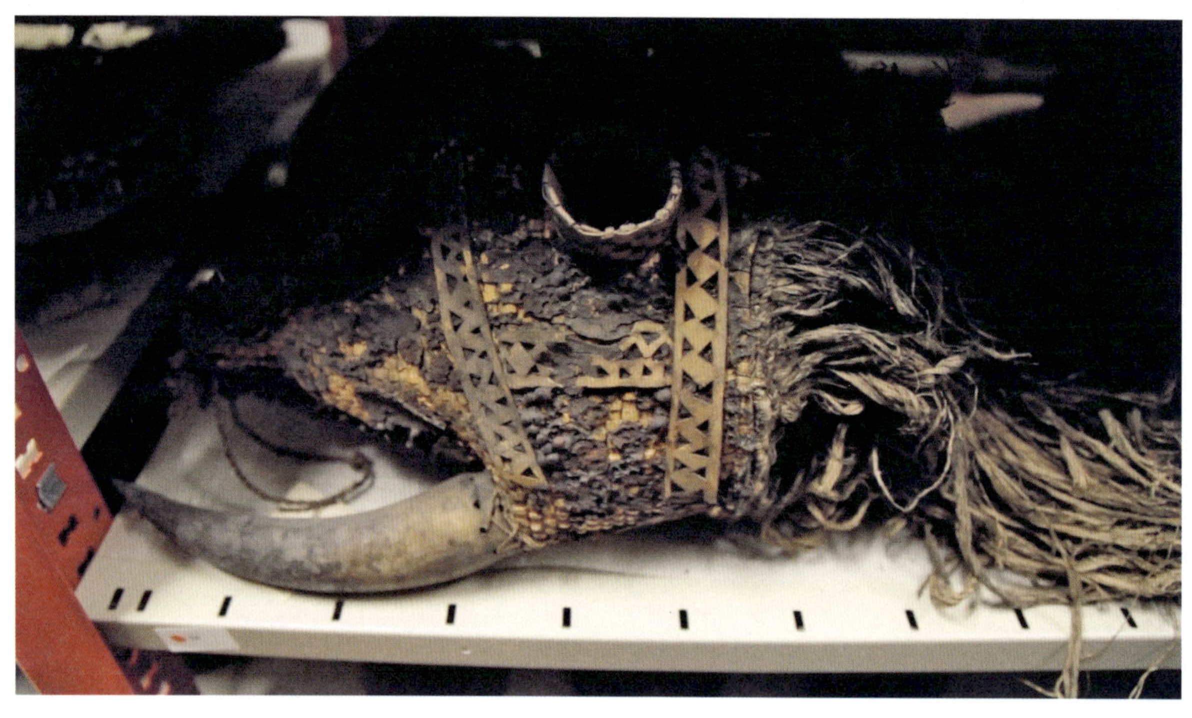

Accumulation Primitive, 2019–2022, video still

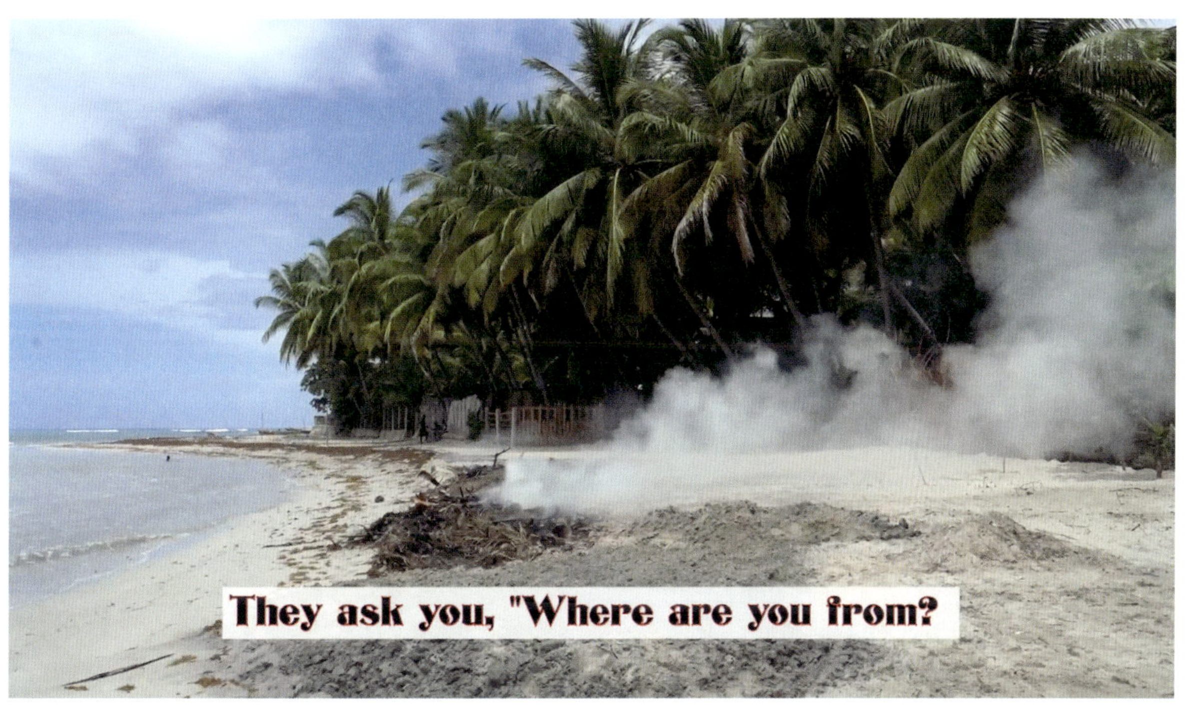

Primitive Amnesia, 2019–2022, video still

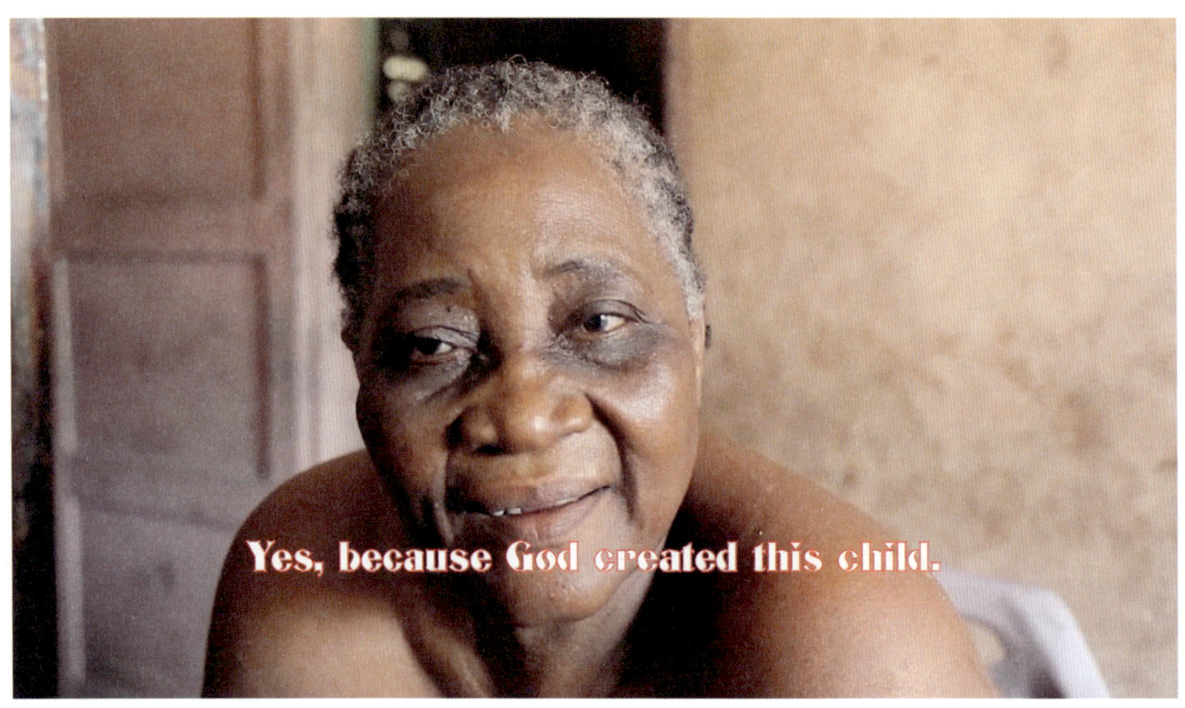

Accumulation Primitive, 2019–2022, video still

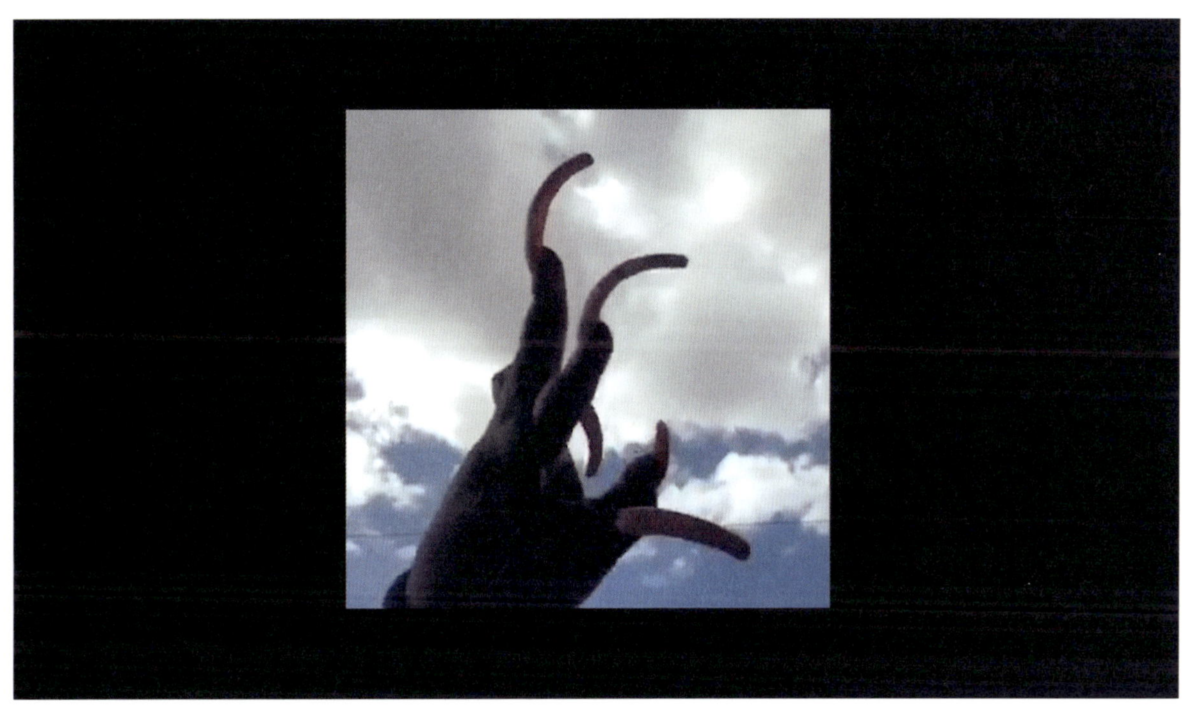

Primitive Amnesia, 2019–2022, video still

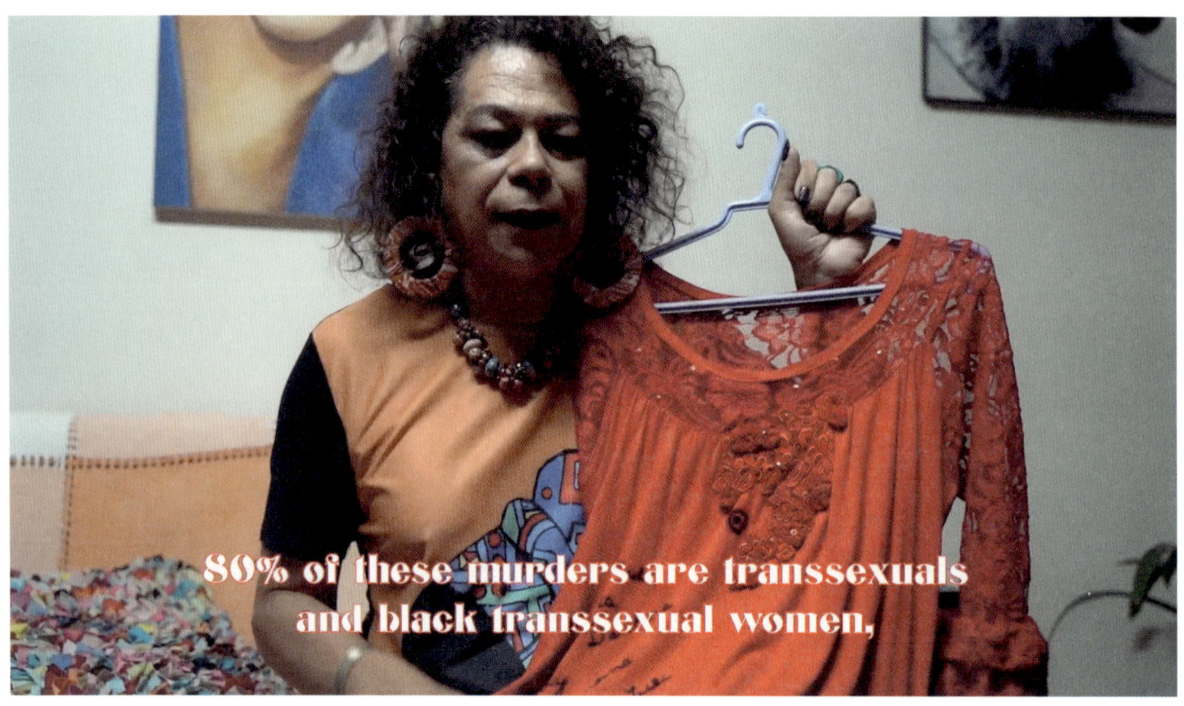

Accumulation Primitive, 2019–2022, video still

Accumulation Primitive

Thomas Conchou

In her film *Accumulation Primitive* (2020), Gaëlle Choisne sets out to meet different women: a herbal healer (the 'leaf doctor') and a voodoo priestess in Haiti, French artist and music producer Christelle Oyiri and her mother, Marie-Carmel Brouard. Their stories intermingle with archival videos, poetic evocations of Haiti and philosophical reflections on the subjugation of women. Through this project, Gaëlle Choisne uses trial and error to search for the emancipatory connections between a collective and personal past and the chaos of the present. By adopting an orphan's position, she builds her own genealogy in which she integrates the capacities of endurance, mutation and transmission of the subjects she represents.

I forgive those who have hurt me in the past and I peacefully distance myself from them: the police, legal systems, the state, racist and heterosexist patriarchal authorities.

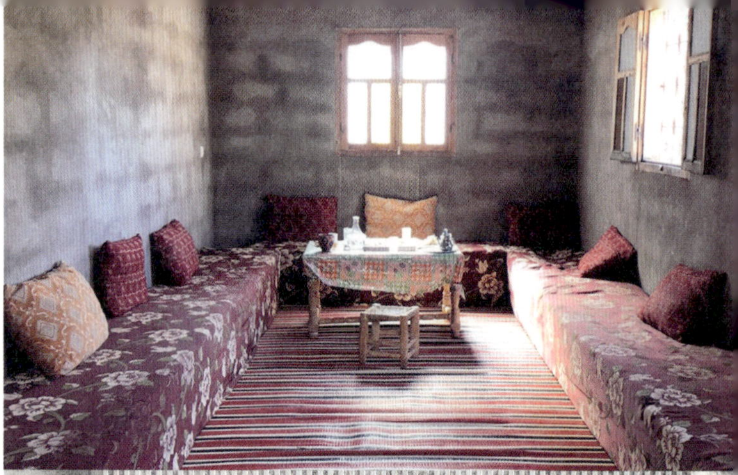

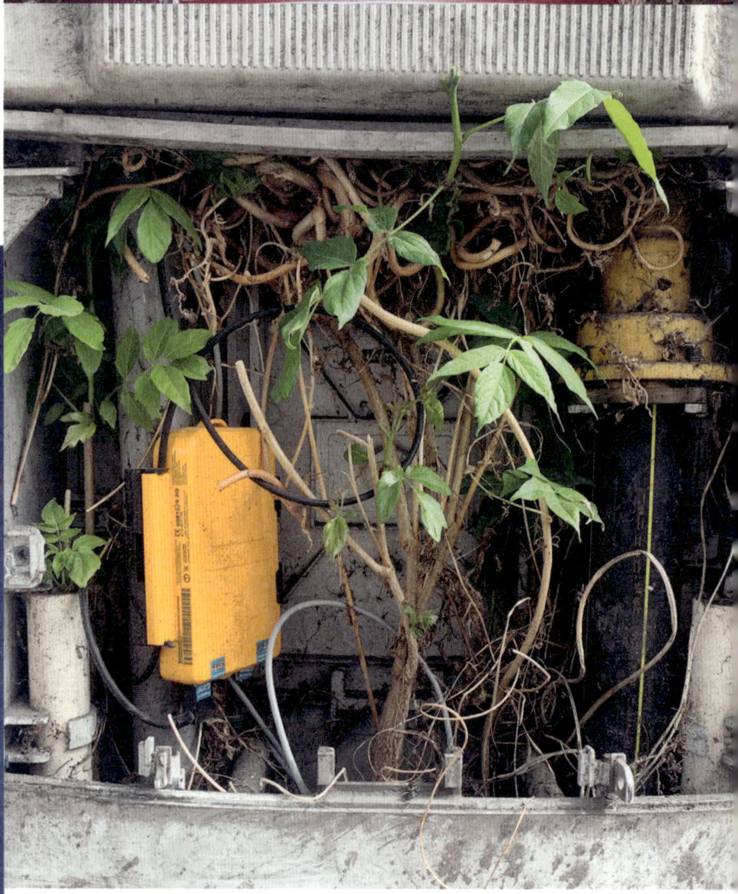

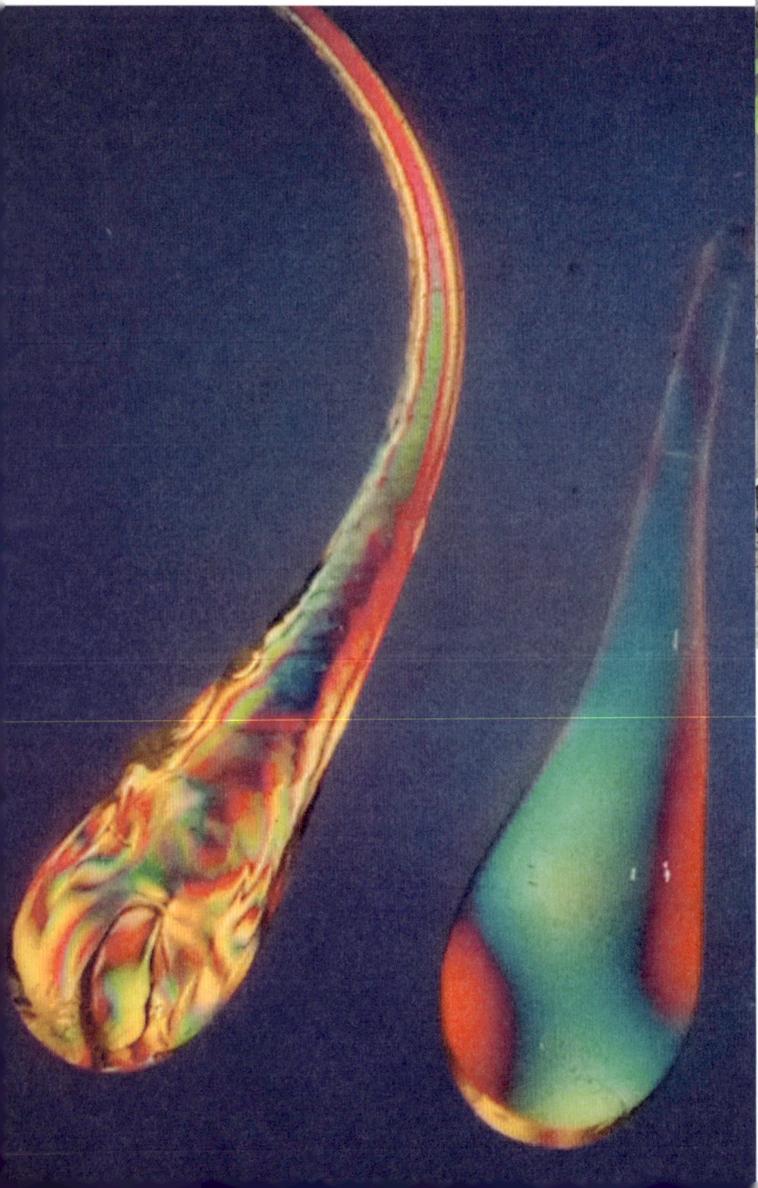

I am brave, and I defend myself against a colonial, sexist, homophobic and transphobic power.

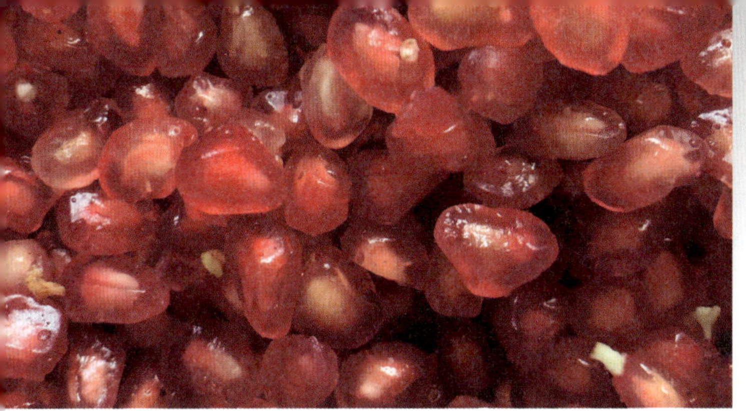

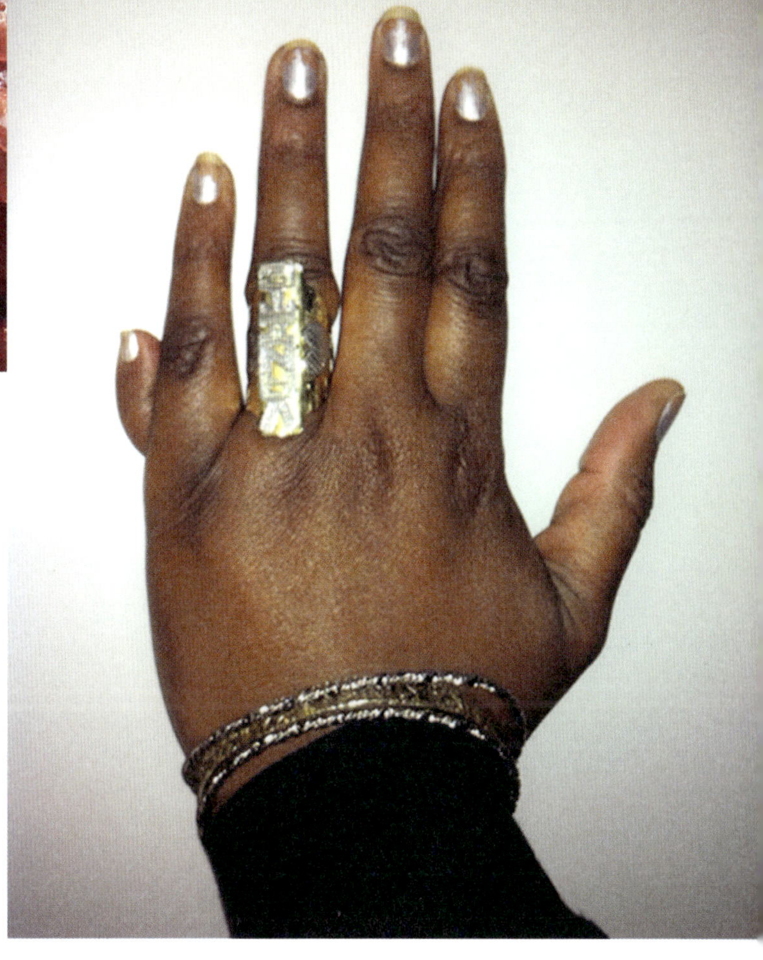

A flow of compassion washes away my rage and replaces it with love for those who are deserving of it: my community, my friends, my sisters, my lovers, people who support and hear me, people who are true to me.

I am wonderful even if the rest of the world leads me to believe otherwise.

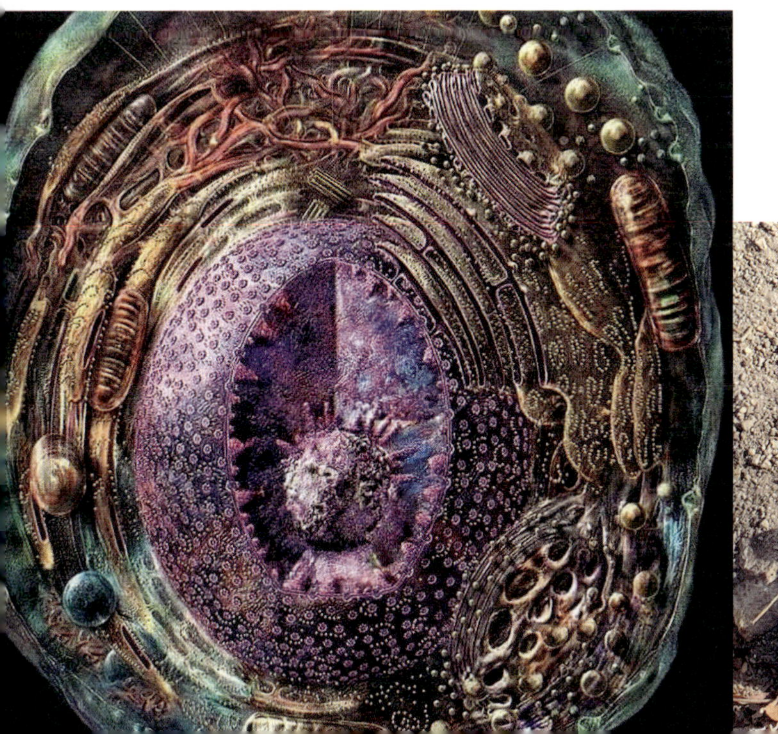

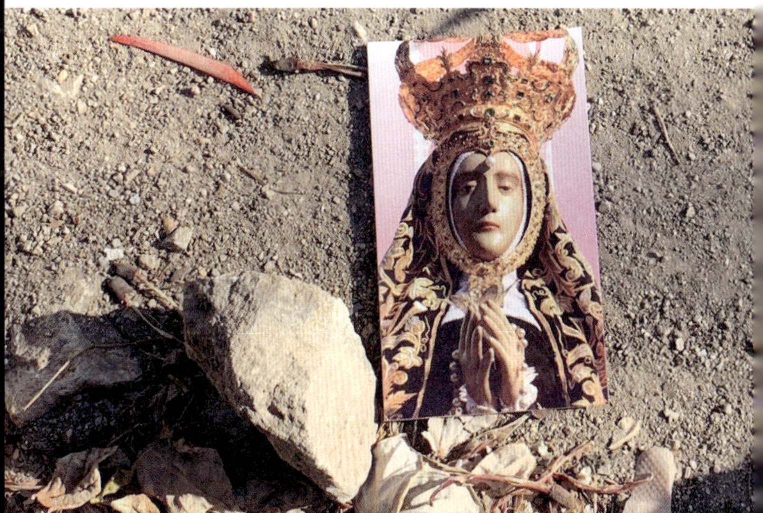

you deserve better

Wong Binghao

Grilled wire fences and disassembled wooden crates delineate a zigzag path through Gaëlle Choisne's installation *Temple of Love – Love to Love*, but this demarcation does little to assuage anxious ambulation, for to worship at this fabulated sanctuary is to feel flushed, flustered, your pulse fluttering. It is as if the installation is oversharing, prematurely obsessing over its temporary inhabitant-paramours, inundating and overwhelming their senses. Not a whiff of commitment phobia here. Perfumed smoke, reminiscent of newborn babies, fresh laundry, cut grass, earthy spices and flowers, permeates these hallowed grounds: an olfactory epitome of 'unconditional love' named *Corps Subtiles* (Subtle Bodies), which the artist created in collaboration with artist Morgan Courtois.[1] A convalescent proposition for the naïve heart. Here and there, piquant sage blunts personally wrapped by the artist pierce the grilles, fortifying layers of aromatic purification for the perambulating enthusiasts of her amorous temple. The crates, previously used to ship the sizeable components of this very work, have been taken apart and annotated, like aspirational mood boards, with the artist's eclectic global image repository of coins, flora and fauna, landmarks and other visual paraphernalia from her travels to Haiti, Brazil and China, alongside internet-sourced archival images from lesbian feminist magazines. Once pregnant with Choisne's work, the crates find new purpose as scaffolds that exuberantly bear her veritable

1 Conversation with the artist via Zoom, November 2021. Email exchanges with the artist, January–June 2022. Gaëlle Choisne uses she/they pronouns; both are used throughout the essay.

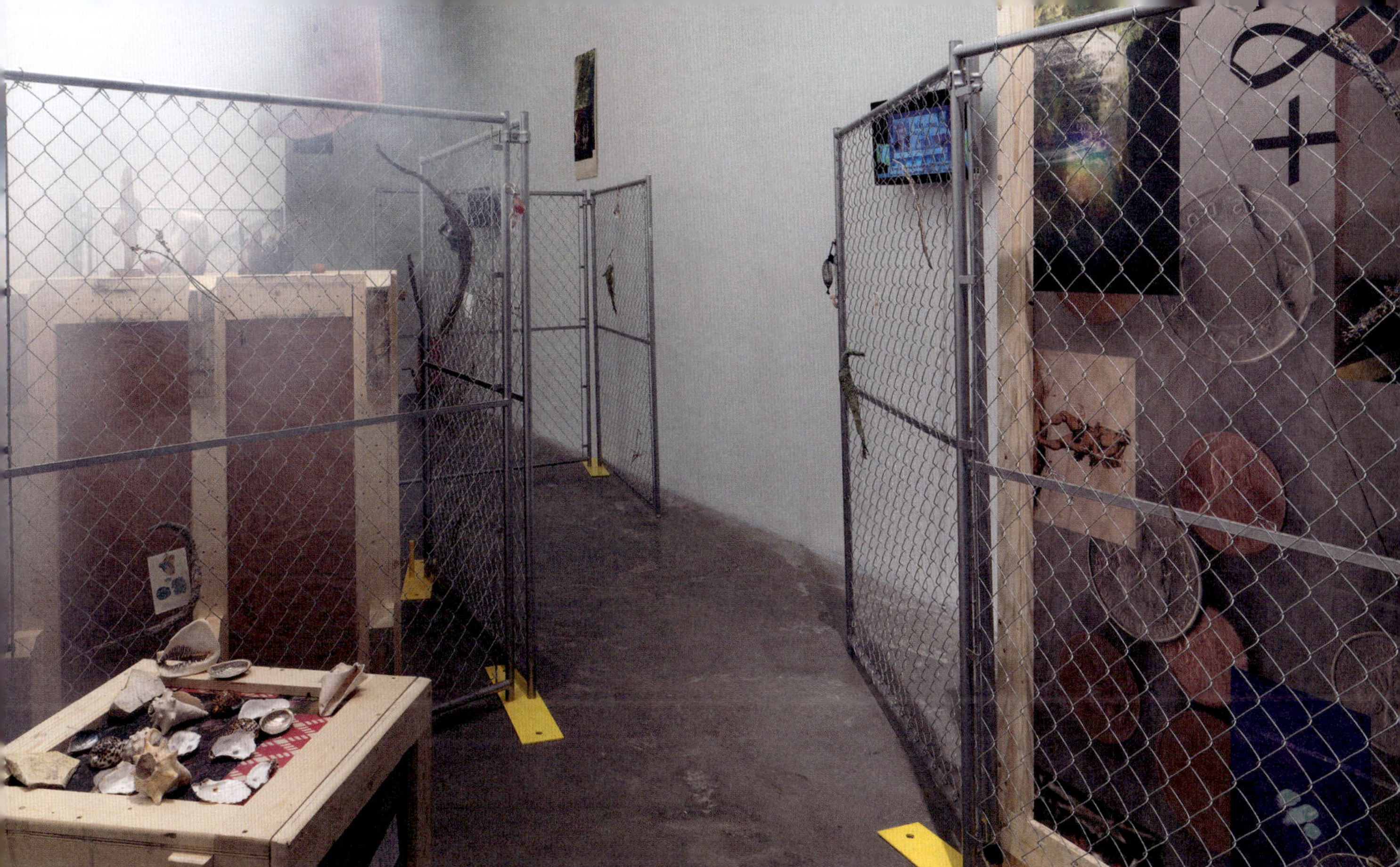

Temple of Love – Love To Love, 2021, exhibition view

visual and tactile banquet, including 3D-printed walnut wood sculptures modelled after Paleolithic Venuses that, in Choisne's words, 'guard the temple', and delicate clusters of seashells onto which poetic, affectionate phrases have been printed.[2]

Snug in a corner of the installation is its figurative altar, what Choisne calls a less-than-utilitarian 'LSD refrigerator'. Onto its curvilinear, purple-lined doors, images, cards and things of varying origins are casually pinned, the single indicator by which it vaguely resembles anything like a used, run-of-the-mill household device. Otherwise, this strange appliance appears to fail its prescribed function of preservation. Its structure is agape, missing the necessary containment; its only protection against kleptomania or atmospheric vagaries is a haphazardly twisted posterior wire mesh that looks like its electrical wires have gone berserk. Apropos of this uncanny edifice, the spattering of fruit and liquid-filled bottles on its shelves appear rotten or else corrupted by alien touch. Overturning our preconceived ideas of domestic serviceability, this outlandish amenity, much like the rest of the installation, ameliorates our emotional conditions more than our material ones. Choisne conceived of this trippy device as a sardonic, oddly self-conscious ego that nudges its users along their paths of soulful nourishment and self-actualisation. Addressing the acolytes of Choisne's love shrine, the ego reads a text written by the artist, in an automated, androgynous rendering of her voice, that acknowledges its own toxic nature. Projected elsewhere in the instal-

2 Ibid.

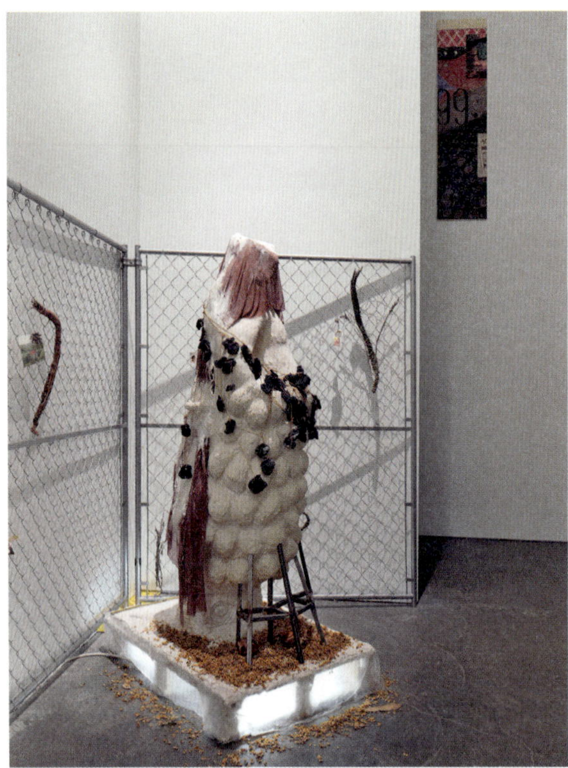

Madone of gratefulness (make a wish and say thank you), 2021

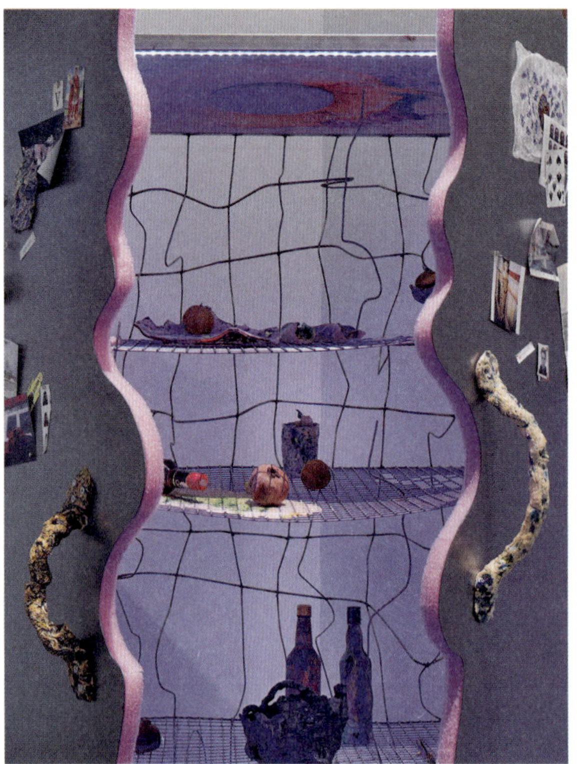

Ego, he goes (Fridge selfspeech and shine love consciousness – Period!), 2021

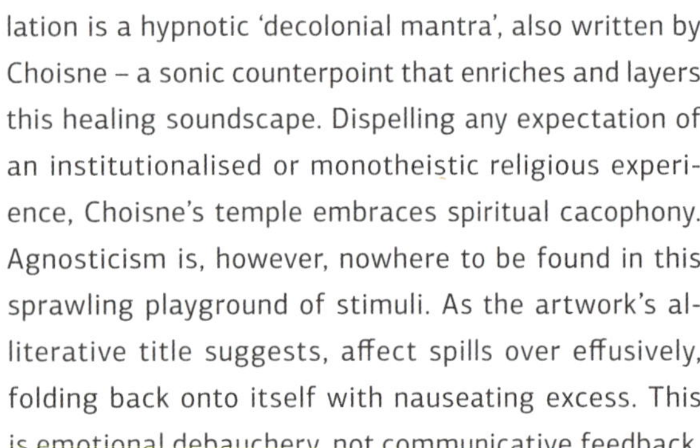

lation is a hypnotic 'decolonial mantra', also written by Choisne – a sonic counterpoint that enriches and layers this healing soundscape. Dispelling any expectation of an institutionalised or monotheistic religious experience, Choisne's temple embraces spiritual cacophony. Agnosticism is, however, nowhere to be found in this sprawling playground of stimuli. As the artwork's alliterative title suggests, affect spills over effusively, folding back onto itself with nauseating excess. This is emotional debauchery, not communicative feedback.

Love to Love is one iteration of an ongoing series of artworks titled *Temple of Love* that Choisne began creating in 2018. To date, there have been thirteen versions and counting, each referencing a chapter from Roland Barthes' *A Lovers' Discourse*. Not quite a literal transference from page to space, Choisne rather imagines their renditions of love as 'a new political ideal' that capaciously enacts and proliferates through strategic conceptual and collaborative 'invitations' to other artists, creatives and political heroes, alive or deceased: her 'luvs'.[3] Choisne's 'post-romantic' horizon of love is 'an inclusive ecosystem' emancipated from the dyadic, zombie-like dogma of compulsory social reproduction. Her off-kilter spaces of kinship and affection generate their own torque, inspiring 'new forms and rituals that might arise beyond the constructs that typically guide and limit aesthetic [and affective] experiences'.[4]

3 Gaëlle Choisne, *Temple of Love* – Manifesto; see p. 8–9. Zoom conversation with the artist, November 2021.

4 Gaëlle Choisne personal portfolio, p. 13.

This modality of expansiveness ports over to Choisne's recent exhibition, *Temple of Love – To Hide*, which features the new video essay *Primitive Accumulation* (2019–2022), in which Choisne intersperses interview footage with femme creatives and healers of colour – such as the anointed 'leaf doctor' Madame Café – with her characteristically heterogeneous references from social media, music videos, news reportage and films. Consider, for instance, a conversation with artist and educator Meg about her paintings and involvement with trans organising in Brazil, which is flanked by excerpts of beauty vlogs, Tierra Whack's music video for 'Unemployed', and rapper Mykki Blanco reciting Zoe Leonard's 1992 poem 'I Want A Dyke For President', among other references. Or voiceovers of a text on the potency of femme eroticism, written by the artist's frequent collaborator Thomas Conchou, overlaid with an ASMR video of silver gel-manicured hands massaging an electric pink loofah, spliced with Cardi B and Megan Thee Stallion's 2020 summer hit 'WAP'. Choisne's subjectivity and artistic method are evident in their careful selections and combinations of seemingly arbitrary material from a worldwide media database in order to 'disrupt documentary, linear and official forms', mirroring her interlocutors' immiscible divinity in the face of extractive greed.[5] Fashioned with a similar approach is *Lie close to your ancestors* (2022), a seven-metre-long carpet – woven by craftswomen from a small village in the Berber mountains near Marrakesh, to whom Choisne was introduced by chance – onto which she appended pins and portraits of inspirational figures, including activists and scholars Audre Lorde and James Baldwin, textile-focused artist Hessie and filmmaker Sarah Maldoror.

For Choisne, these sundry sources and histories are intimately ribboned to each other and her artworks, despite not displaying any immediately identifiable or direct links to either.[6] Their artistic approach is a panacea to what historian Sanjay Subrahmanyam calls the encroaching 'parochialism' of area studies (or epistemology writ large), wherein 'conventional [geographical] units of analysis, fortuitously defined [and created] as givens for the intellectually slothful… somehow become real and overwhelming'.[7] Against this sort of deadening faux uniformity, Choisne's self-described 'kaleidoscopic' methodology unearths latent connections between unexpected worlds, forging pathways to escape the consolidation of power and intellectual borders.

To hide from love, in Barthes' formulation, reeks of the luxury of petulant navel-gazing; solitude misused. Articulating what he calls the 'double discourse' or 'active paradox' of passion, in which the lover procedurally and neurotically plots for a loved object's attention while desperately trying not to concede too much of their own affections, Barthes describes an anxious lover who 'tergiversate[s]', hesitates, desires to be 'both pathetic and admirable' in their gambit for romantic affirmation despite the ever-present risk of rejection.[8] The privileged perils of conventional courtship rituals are aspirational as much as they are traps. Of the roiling loneliness in trans experiences of love, Janet Mock writes in her memoir: 'In rare moments of self-reflection, when faced with no one but myself, I dropped the mask… I recognised me and often chose to dismiss her with the one question that pushed me to put the mask back on: Who will ever love you if you tell the truth?'[9] The metaphorical mask that Mock once used to hide from the possibility of love is the same device that enabled her to confront love's ruthless refusals and confiscations. It is also the apparatus that she deployed to survive love's game, an ordeal that one imagines would resolutely silence Barthes' petty protagonist.

5 Conversation with the artist via Zoom, May 2022.

6 Ibid.

7 Sanjay Subrahmanyam, 'Connected Histories: Notes Towards a Reconfiguration of Early Modern Eurasia', *Modern Asian Studies*, vol. 31, no. 3, July 1997, pp. 742–743.

8 Roland Barthes, *A Lover's Discourse: Fragments*, trans. Richard Howard, New York: Hill and Wang, 1978, pp. 41–43.

9 Janet Mock, *Redefining Realness: My Path to Womanhood, Identity, Love & So Much More*, New York: Atria Books, 2014, pp. 72–74.

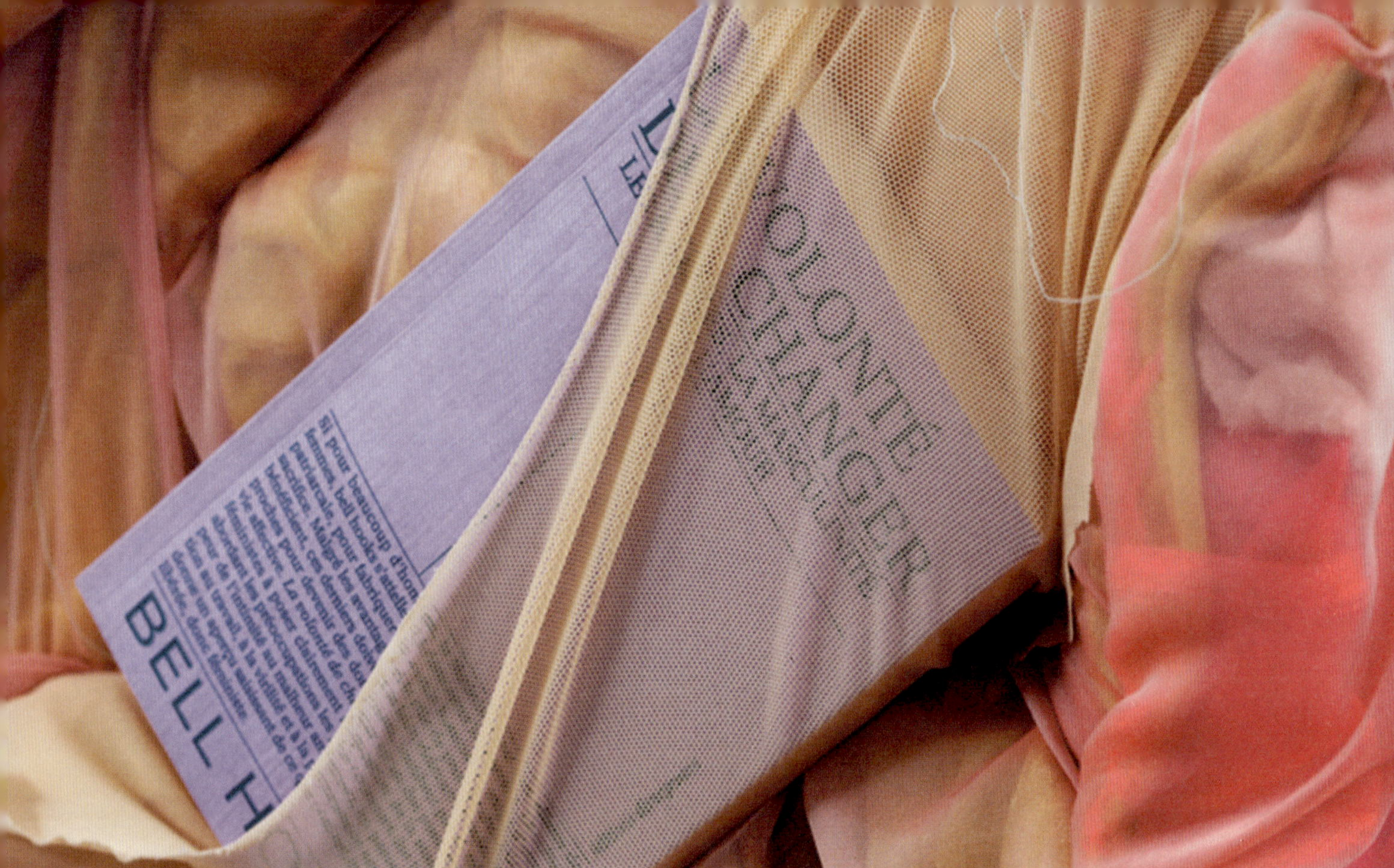

Textus (detail), 2018–2022

The politics of love, as elaborated by Choisne or Mock, is hardly characterised by insularity or misanthropy, just a differently textured relationality. Since they were a child, Choisne inquisitively and instinctively collected miscellaneous items that were discarded in public spaces and streets. She would also scour street and flea markets for inexpensive trinkets that caught her eye. Although these items were admittedly unrelated ('It doesn't make sense to collect these things!'), Choisne began noticing loose patterns and proclivities in her vast, years-long repository of shabby, scavenged objects.[10] Besides a handful of rare and special finds are recurring and comparatively ordinary objects such as seashells, coins, keys, locks, plastic bags, cigarettes and playing cards (to date, the artist has assembled an almost complete deck).[11] Choisne believes that these 'periods' of seemingly random interests throughout their personal and artistic lives are 'never a coincidence', but rather 'fragments that suddenly come together', disperse and repeat themselves in other artworks,[12] recalling what performance theorist André Lepecki calls the 'will to archive' in relation to dance re-enactments in contemporary art: a vitality that seeks to 'unlock, release, and actualize' in a (past) work 'still non-exhausted creative fields' and virtual possibilities.[13] For Lepecki, this act of harking back is neither nostalgic nor

10 Studio visit with the artist, Berlin, June 2022.

11 Ibid. Of note are an alluring lenticular print depicting a pair of majestic unicorns galloping through a rainbow-crested waterfall, and an Egyptian blue and gold metal box emblazoned with an intricate astrology chart.

12 Studio visit, June 2022.

13 André Lepecki, 'The Body as Archive: Will to Re-Enact and the Afterlives of Dance', *Dance Research Journal*, vol. 42, no. 2, Winter 2010, p. 31.

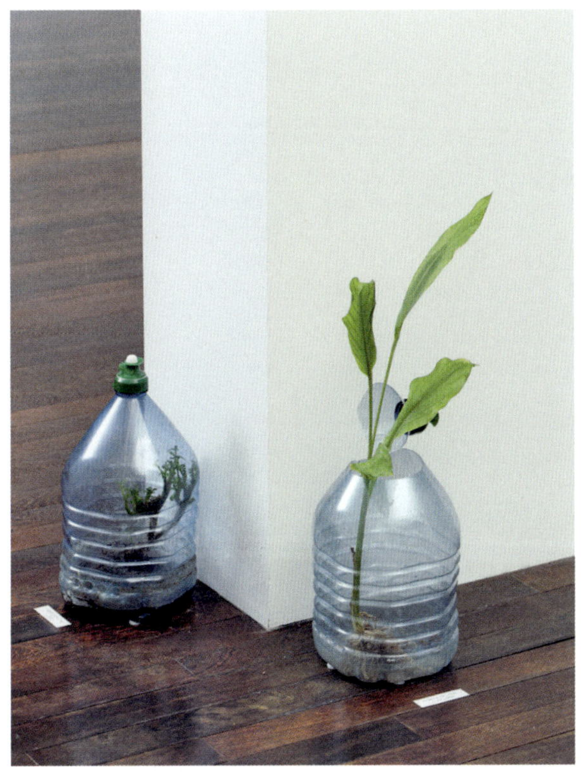

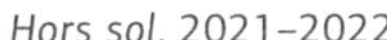
Hors sol, 2021–2022

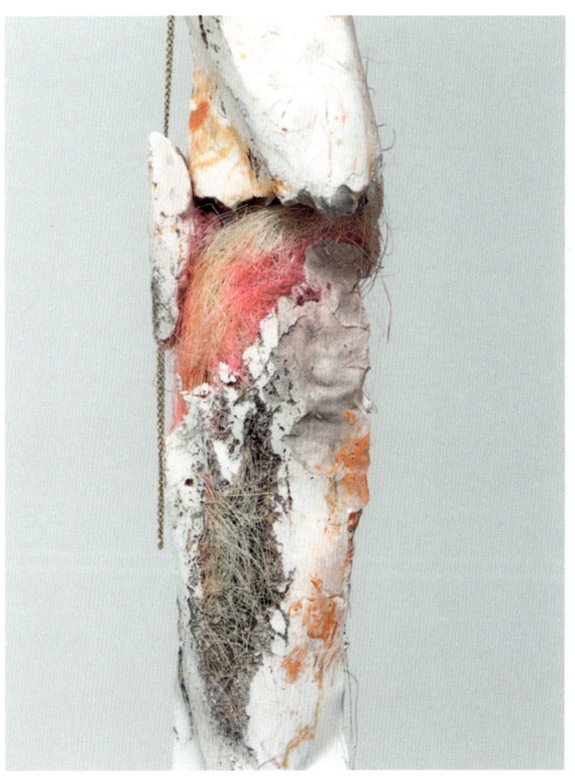

Potomitan (detail), 2021–2022

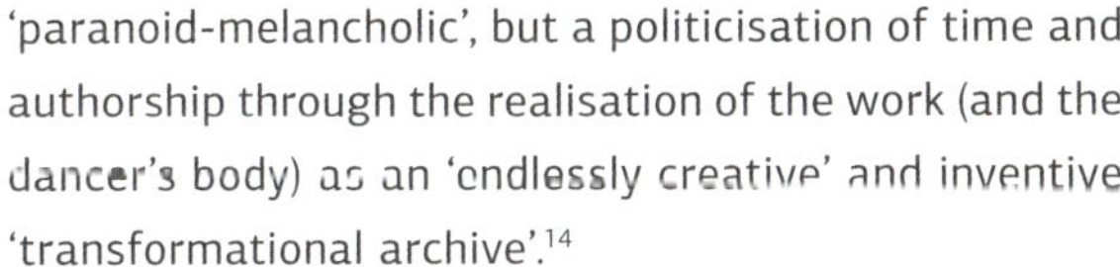
'paranoid-melancholic', but a politicisation of time and authorship through the realisation of the work (and the dancer's body) as an 'endlessly creative' and inventive 'transformational archive'.[14]

Similarly enriched with the open sum of her life experiences, Choisne's curio collections serve as the 'unconscious background' and genesis for an artistic corpus of visceral, multi-sensory aggregations that shuns didactic and regimented frameworks.[15] Most notably, Choisne makes 'charms' – typically ornamented, stuffed and scented fabric sacs of varying sizes which are a significant component in most of their artworks – by intuitively sewing, attaching and combining various articles from her impressive treasury.[16] 'Charged' to 'heal people' and 'create new perspectives', Choisne's charms act like solvents, exemplifying her embodied ability to intuitively sublimate – without uniformising – ostensibly banal and incompatible entities, be they material, affective or intellectual.[17] But hers is not a methodologically rigid or regularising touch: her objects retain their kitschy odours and protuberances within the terrains of their respective assemblages. Choisne's charms remain formally and conceptually indecipherable. They are not prescriptions for transcendence. 'Matter', as art historian K. Yoshida argues, is 'not a great ontological unifier', but 'paradoxically [that which] relates the subject to the world through doubt, not

14 Lepecki, p. 46.

15 Studio visit, June 2022.

16 Ibid. Subtle Bodies, the fragrance of 'unconditional love' used in *Temple of Love – Love to Love*, is also used to perfume the charms.

17 Studio visit, June 2022.

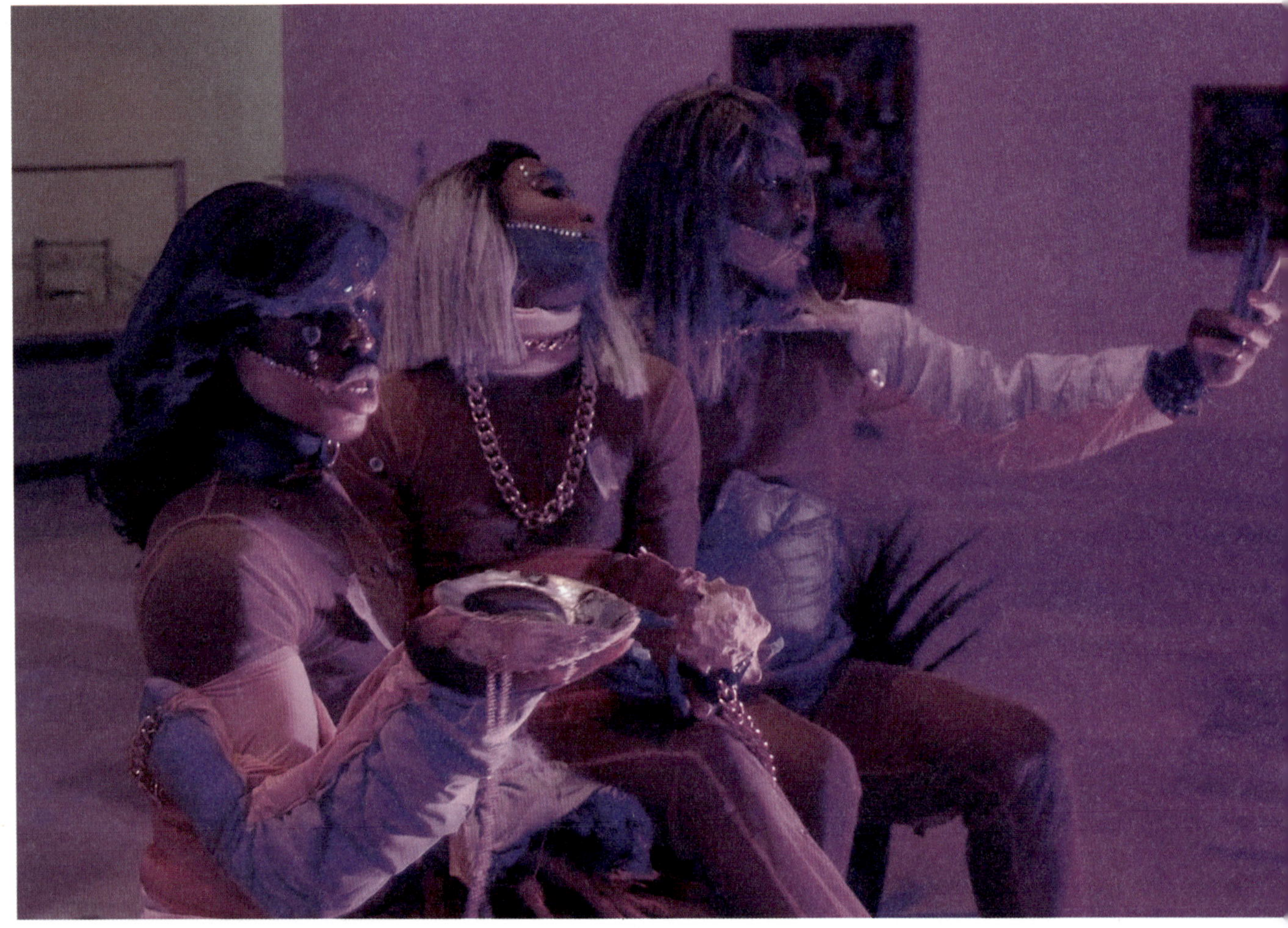

Performance of *Temple of Love – Affirmation*, 2020, project in collaboration with HOUSE OF NINJA, Nuit Blanche, Musée d'Art Moderne de la Ville de Paris, France

trust', through opacity, not transparency.[18] Against demagogical demands for total access and connection in post-war Japan, a precondition for the possession and homogenisation of knowledge, population and territory, Yoshida proposes the 'non-dominance', opacity and obtuseness of 'irrelation'. On the irreversibly hermetic black boxes in Kawagachi Tatsuo and Muraoka Saburo's artworks, for example, Yoshida describes an art that 'communicates… separation if only to impart excessive abundance that belongs to no one', confounding and eluding maker and viewer alike.[19] Although Choisne thinks of her charms as 'portals to other invisible worlds', what and where these worlds are, how we might get there, and why they matter to us, are not questions that she necessarily wants to, or can, answer on behalf of the spectators of her artworks.[20] Love gives and gives, but it does not spoon-feed.

18 K. Yoshida, *Avant-Garde Art and Non-dominant Thought in Postwar Japan: Image, Matter, Separation*, New York: Routledge, 2021, p. 56.

19 Yoshida, p. 218.

20 Studio visit, June 2022.

This might be what theorists Laurent Berlant and Michael Hardt had in mind when thinking through love's 'non-sovereignty': how it necessitates 'becom[ing] different' through desiring 'incommensurate things' and consequently, echoing Choisne's creative impulses, 'violating your own attachment to your intentionality, without being anti-intentional'.[21] That love's only guarantee is 'change without guarantees' signals that its enactment of relationality is never a benign participatory Bourriaudian show.[22] Love, not without a pinch of cloying irony, can transform your essence, if you let it.

From January to December 2022, Choisne's *Temple of Love – Atopos* acts as an exhibition within an exhibition at MAC VAL Museum, located in a southern suburb of Paris. *Atopos* consists of about 20 portable and 'functional' sculptures – including a piece that can be used as a massage table and another for dance – which are exhibited alongside the museum's current collection display.[23] Encouraging the particularities of local public engagement, the sculptures will be activated through Choisne's curatorial interventions in the museum's public programme calendar, demonstrating once again her ability to grasp and offset the edifices that she inhabits. In a somewhat uncharacteristic move, Barthes describes *atopos*, or 'without discourse', as an 'unclassifiable… ceaselessly unforeseen originality' that is found in the 'relation' between a loved being and amorous subject, between the other and I.[24] *Atopos* cannot be possessed or dictated. Quite the contrary, its original relation is precisely that which 'shake[s], transcend[s]' and 'evacuate[s]' the 'injuries' of love's 'stereotype[s]', such as a fierce jealousy or frustration in the face of neglect.[25]

I argue that these unorthodox and unpredictable qualities of association – between things, territories, feelings, ideas, bodies and publics – are at the heart of Choisne's artistic approach. It should therefore come as no surprise that they think of their artworks as quirky assemblages.[26] Theorist Jasbir K. Puar motions assemblage as a supplement to intersectional identities, the latter of which, she contends, are 'the by-product of attempts to still and quell the perpetual motion' and 'threatening mobility' of assemblages.[27] Prioritising process over product, liminal bodily matter over its seamless identity formulations, assemblage shows how controlled societies act 'not predominantly through signification or identity interpellation but rather through affective capacities and tendencies',[28] echoing Berlant and Hardt's debate that love 'makes central the role of affect within the political sphere'.[29] Love's seduction is its abstract danger.

To love – according to Barthes, skyrocketing love scams and too many Hinge dates – is more often than not to lose oneself, to be engulfed,[30] to waste one's time and patience,[31] to be jealous, histrionic and emotionally distraught,[32] to give selfishly, not selflessly, all in the name of an ideological fantasy.[33] Love is an untenable contract with an ungraspable idol that promises few benefits and demands too many conditions. What Choisne's artworks do is to 'show the limits we have created by ourselves' in our relationships with life and love.[34] 'We all try to be happy,' the artist tells me in their Berlin studio, 'but we don't know what else is [out]

21 Heather Davis and Paige Sarlin, 'No One Is Sovereign in Love: A Conversation Between Lauren Berlant and Michael Hardt', *No More Potlucks*, no. 18, December 2011, accessed via http://coalition.org.mk/archives/646?lang=en.

22 Ibid.

23 Conversation with the artist via Zoom, November 2021.

24 Barthes, pp. 34–35.

25 Ibid., pp. 35–36.

26 Studio visit, June 2022.

27 Jasbir K. Puar, '"I would rather be a cyborg than a goddess." Becoming-Intersectional in Assemblage Theory', *philoSOPHIA State University of New York Press*, vol. 2, no. 1, 2012, pp. 49–50.

28 Puar, pp. 56, 63.

29 Davis and Sarlin.

30 Barthes, p. 10.

31 Ibid., pp. 13, 37, 39–40.

32 Ibid., pp. 65–66, 110, 144.

33 Ibid., pp. 41–44, 181–182.

34 Studio visit, June 2022.

there.'[35] Another pertinent axiom from Barthes: 'to *want* to be pigeonholed is to want to obtain for life a docile reception'.[36] Barthes' intention here is easily comprehended, but I would like to focus on the charge of the word 'want', iterated twice for emphasis. To want is to desire, or to indicate, an entity that one does not yet have. Why would anyone, as Barthes implies, want to have a boring, ineffectual life or an uninteresting love? He offers that it is the 'power' of systems and structures of intimacy that makes them covetable.[37]

Thinking through the possibilities for American feminist art, curator and art historian Helen Molesworth writes that 'we are witnessing the replacement of the either/or logic of the dialectic with the conjunction "and"' which is 'not the language of the inevitable but the contingent, wobbling our routine spatiotemporal conventions, shying away from the hard-and-fast language of causality'.[38] The iterative force of 'and' gestures towards a different sort of power that is neither envious nor calculative, kind of like what love *should* be. A propulsion into the unknown, the staggering dynamism of 'and' disconcerts tepid existential moulds. Choisne's artworks can be thought of as sequences of 'ands'; in other words, situationships. Just without the toxicity.

35 Ibid.

36 Barthes, p. 46.

37 Ibid., 47.

38 Helen Molesworth, 'How to Install Art as a Feminist', in *Modern Women: Women Artists at the Museum of Modern Art*, eds. Cornelia Butler and Alexandra Schwartz, New York: The Museum of Modern Art, 2010, p. 510.

Wong Binghao approaches art through curatorial and essayistic modes. They constellate contextually specific, conceptually capacious and emotionally available readings and experiences of art in the hope of more emancipatory and ethical worlds. They are currently C-MAP Asia Fellow for the Museum of Modern Art.

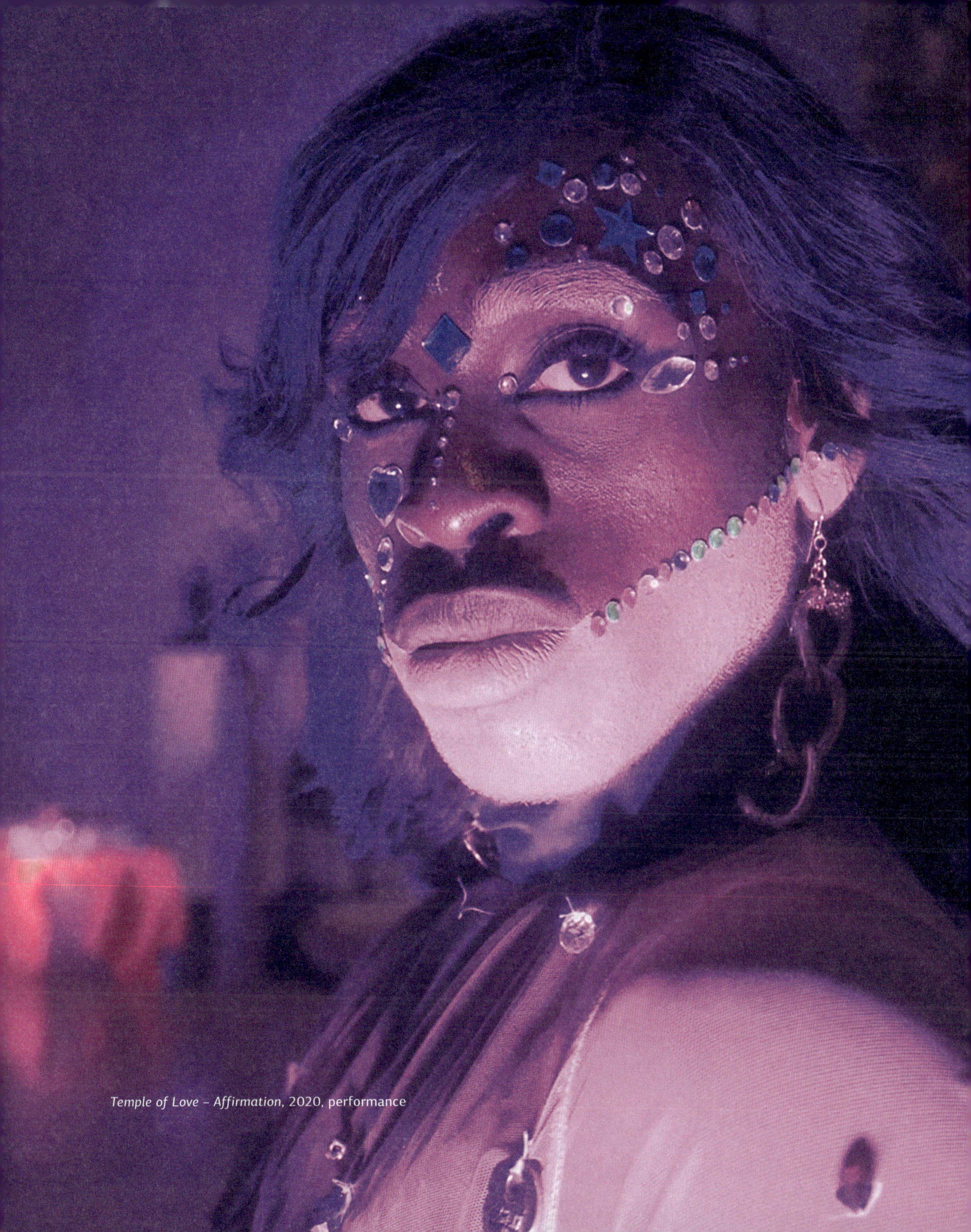

Temple of Love – Affirmation, 2020, performance

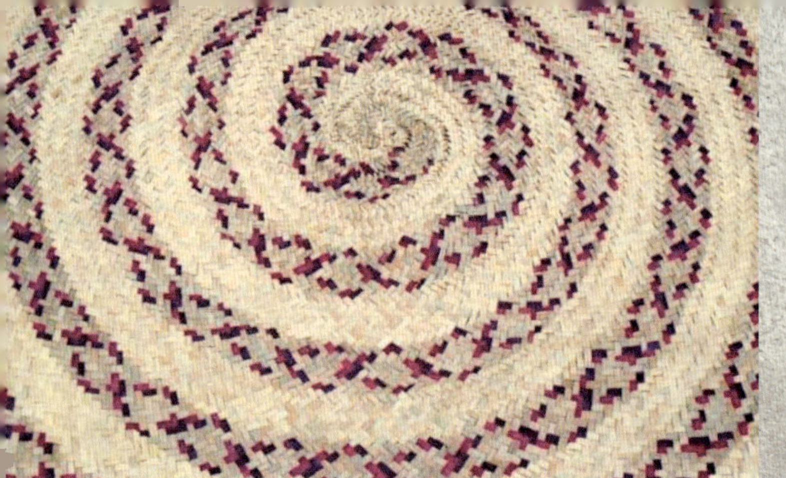

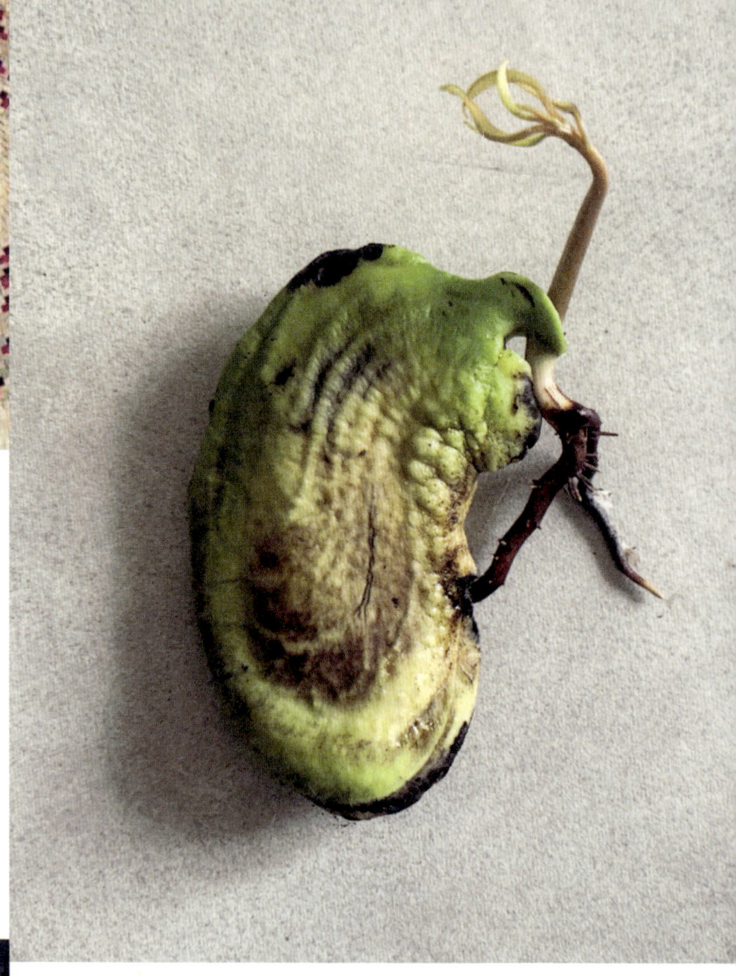

I have a strong sense of self-worth, even though I have no role model. I become my own role model.

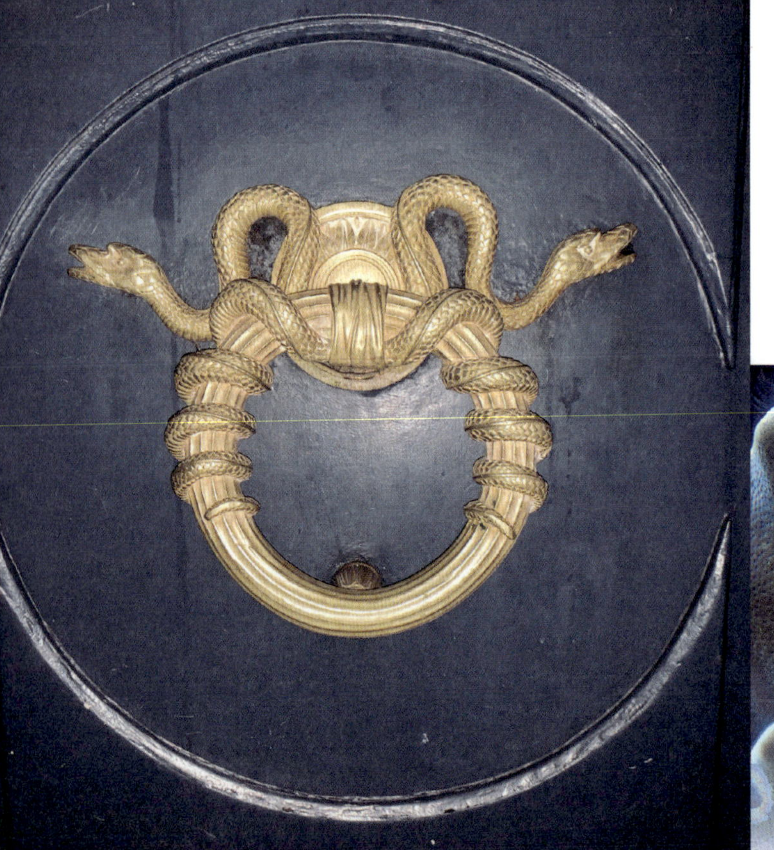

Hard times are short-lived; they are trials and tribulations.

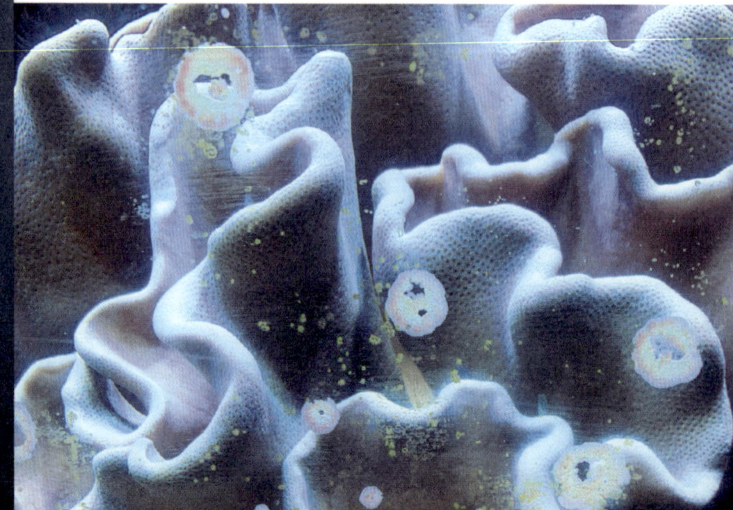

I must create an ideal and live up to it: no more injustices, no more theft, no more rape, no more violence against human and non-human beings.

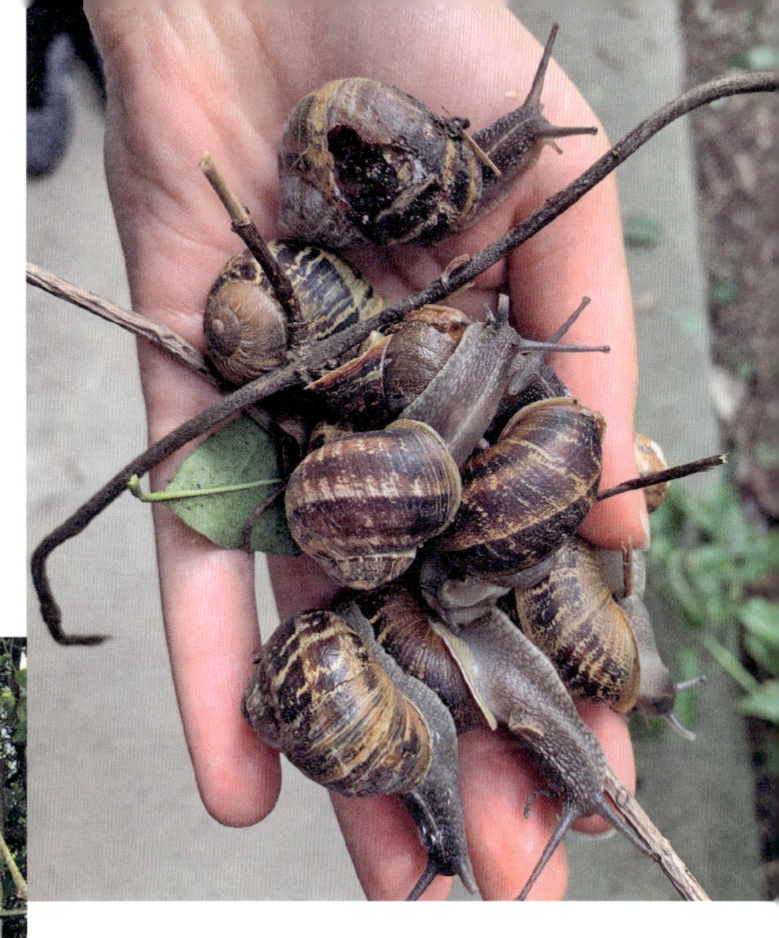

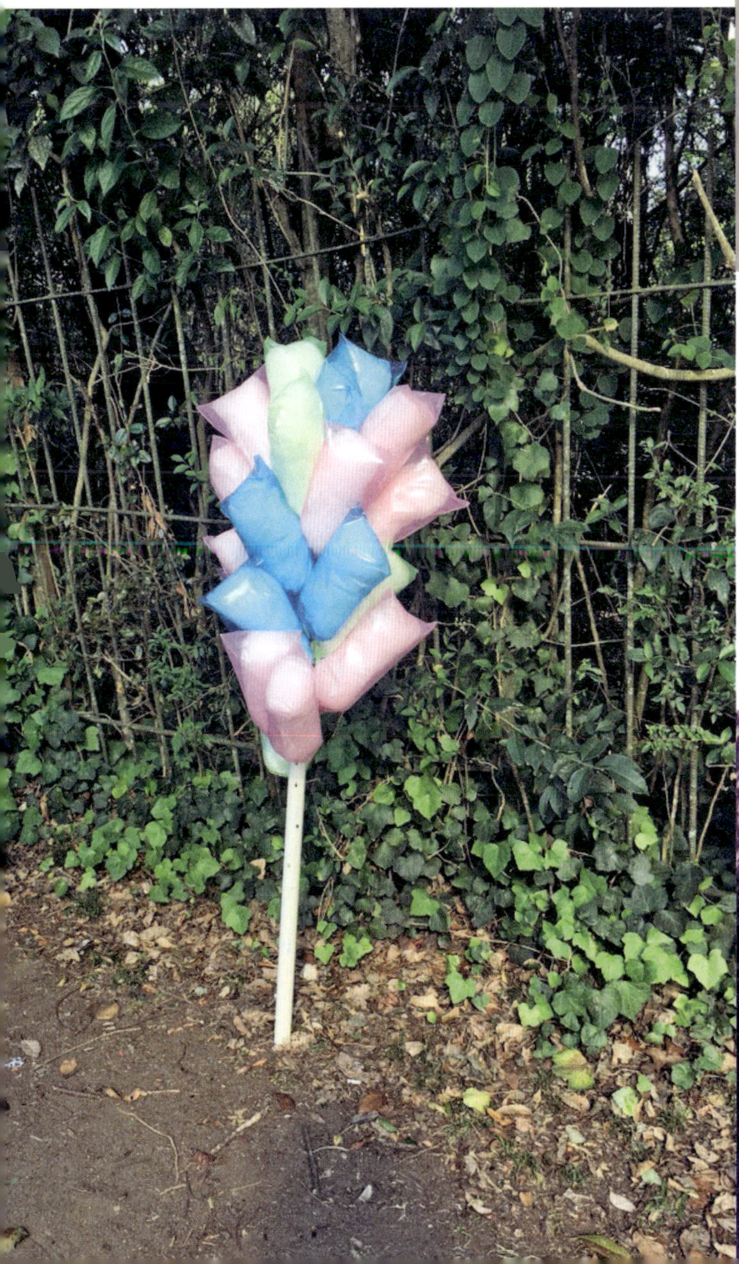

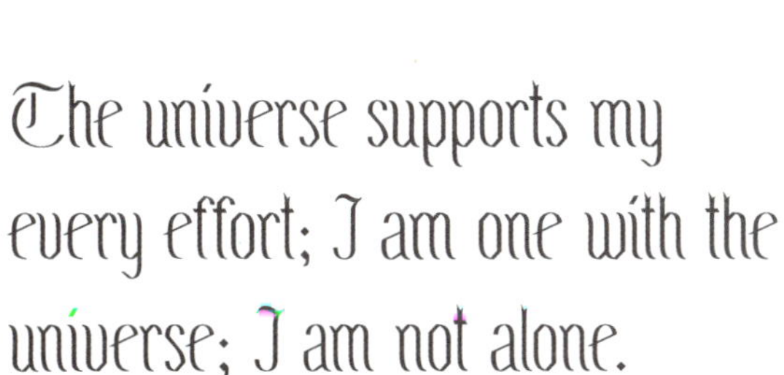

The universe supports my every effort; I am one with the universe; I am not alone.

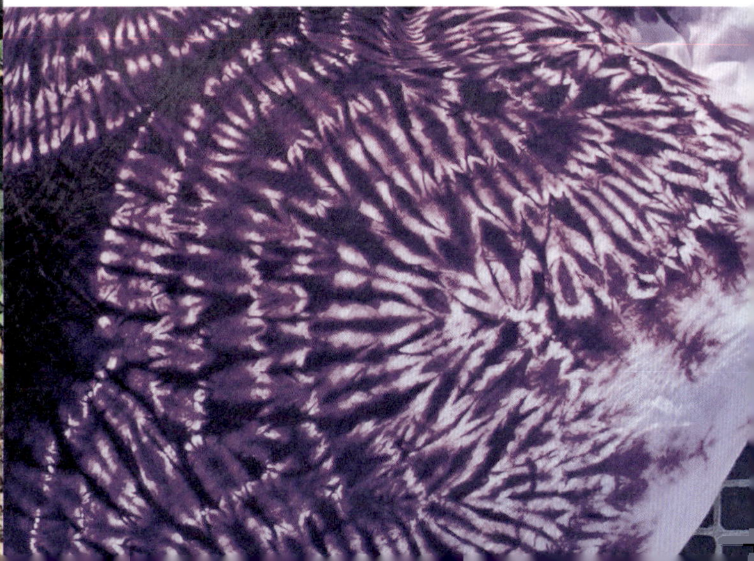

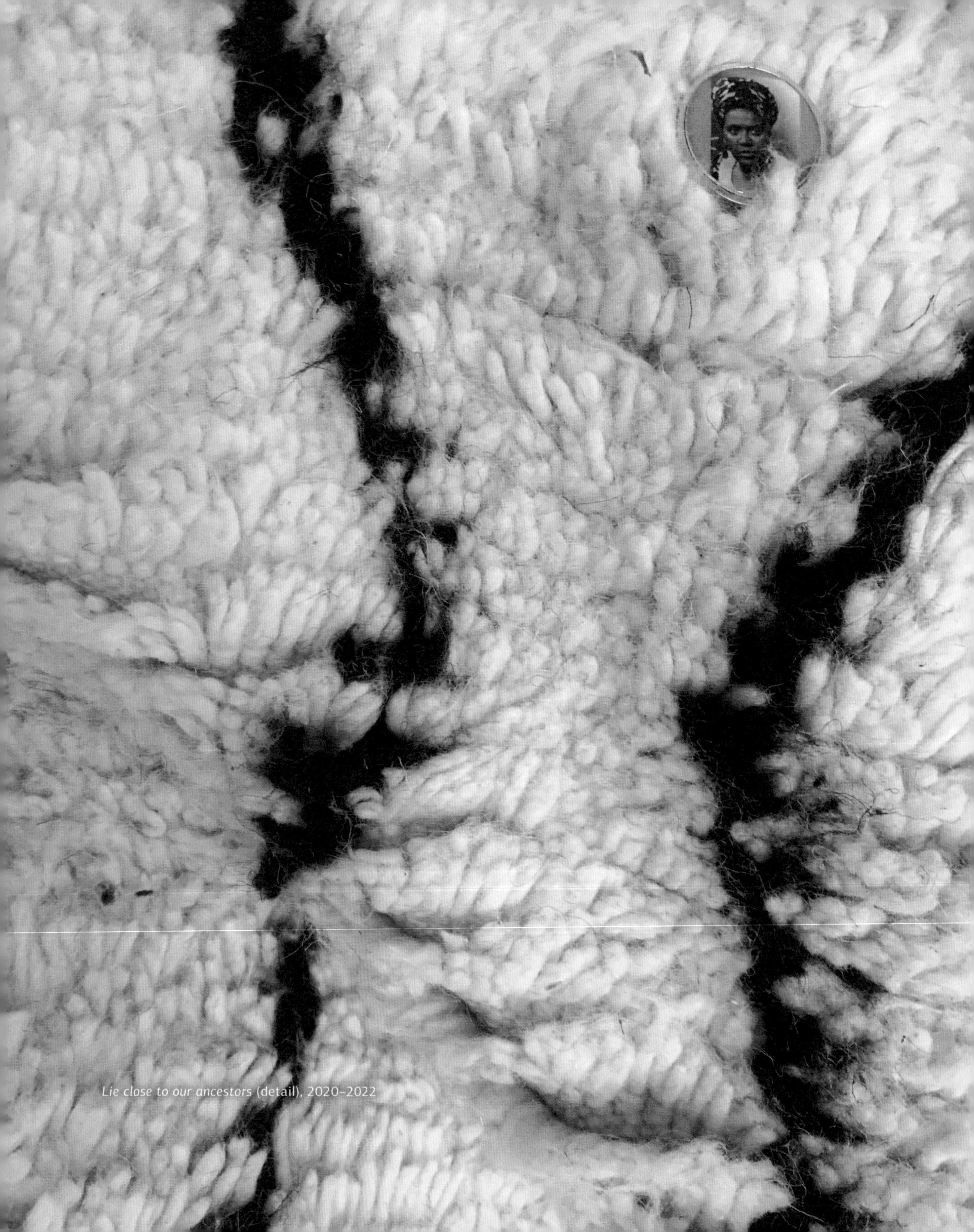

Lie close to our ancestors (detail), 2020–2022

The Desert

Djibril Sall

I come to in a dream – a little black boy walking the red desert to the horizon. To the left of him is the moon and to the right is the sun, squeezing the sky and all its stars into liminal spaces. No shoes. Just bare feet to meet the hot sand, the smell of burning soles and a dry breeze sucking moisture out of skin clinging to his ankles. Or is it mine? At the event horizon stands a black girl who is five in a dress just as old, her ebony skin stops at her ankles and her feet become ivory. The little black boy blinks three times and opens his eyes to stand next to her. Her teeth are dazzling white, her tongue as pink as Lake Retba and she smiles, 'your dream has been waiting for you'.

I tiptoe to take a closer look at her eyes and an endless pit expands from her pupils to the corners of her sclera. The little black boy falls into the universe of her left eye and the desert grows dark. I come to on top of a plateau of a great pyramid. There is no sun, no moon, no stars, no girl. Just clouds that shift between grey and purple and countless pyramids stretching into the expanse of the Sahel. Coming to the edge, the little black boy jumps from 10,000 metres onto the sand below. He hears his bones crunching at his ankles. He stands and walks up the stairs to the top of the same pyramid. Then he jumps down again. And again. And again. And again for the passing of eternity. I wake up to find my legs tingling under the cover of my white bedsheets.

This is not a dream. This is the universe. I am reminded of the time my mother took me into the desert to visit a holy man. That night I slept outside with my cousin and uncle and marvelled at how I can see every star in existence. The following day the holy man called on Allah, spat on my forehead three times, and then gave me a bucket of magic water to bathe in. I emptied the bucket above my head but still didn't know who or what I needed protection from. I asked my mother why and she baptised me in the depravity of the world. Evil tongues, evil eyes, demons calling your true name at noon, the denizens of midnight, Débo Bismillah who lives at the bottom of the lake, and her fingers are blades.

Extract from Djibril Sall's reading for the opening of *Temple of Love – To Hide*, Künstlerhaus Bethanien, Berlin, Germany, 19 May 2022.

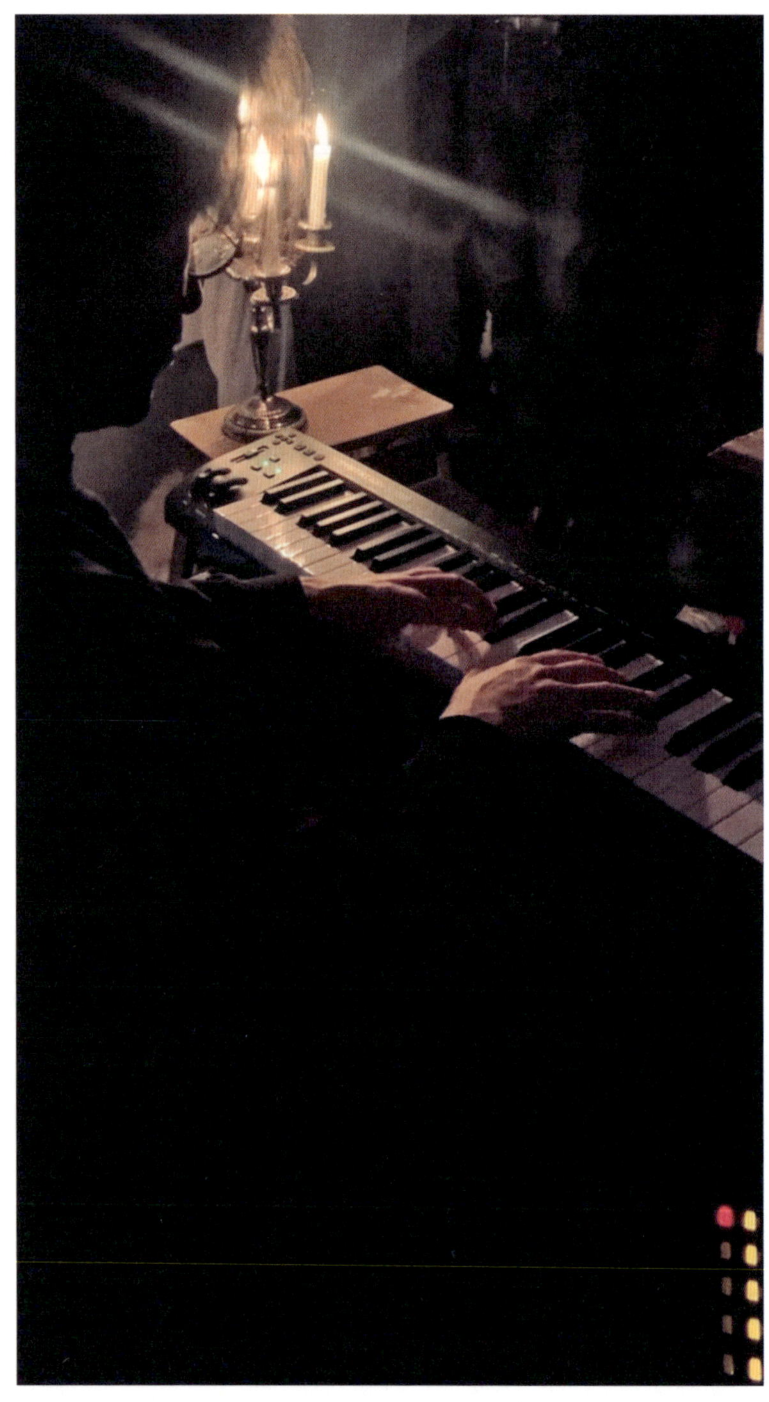

Portraits of Pablo Altar (left) and Djibril Sall (right) prior to their performance for the opening of *Temple of Love – To Hide*

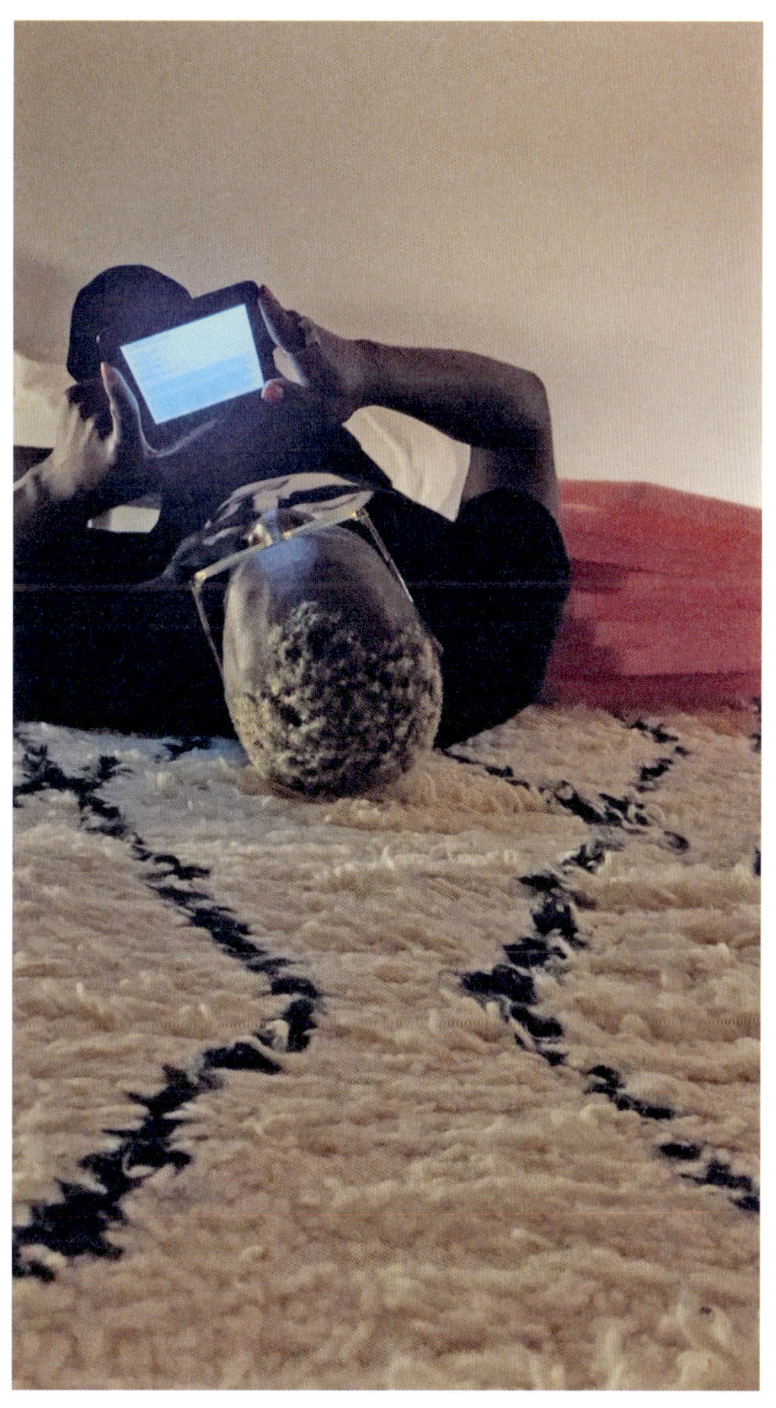

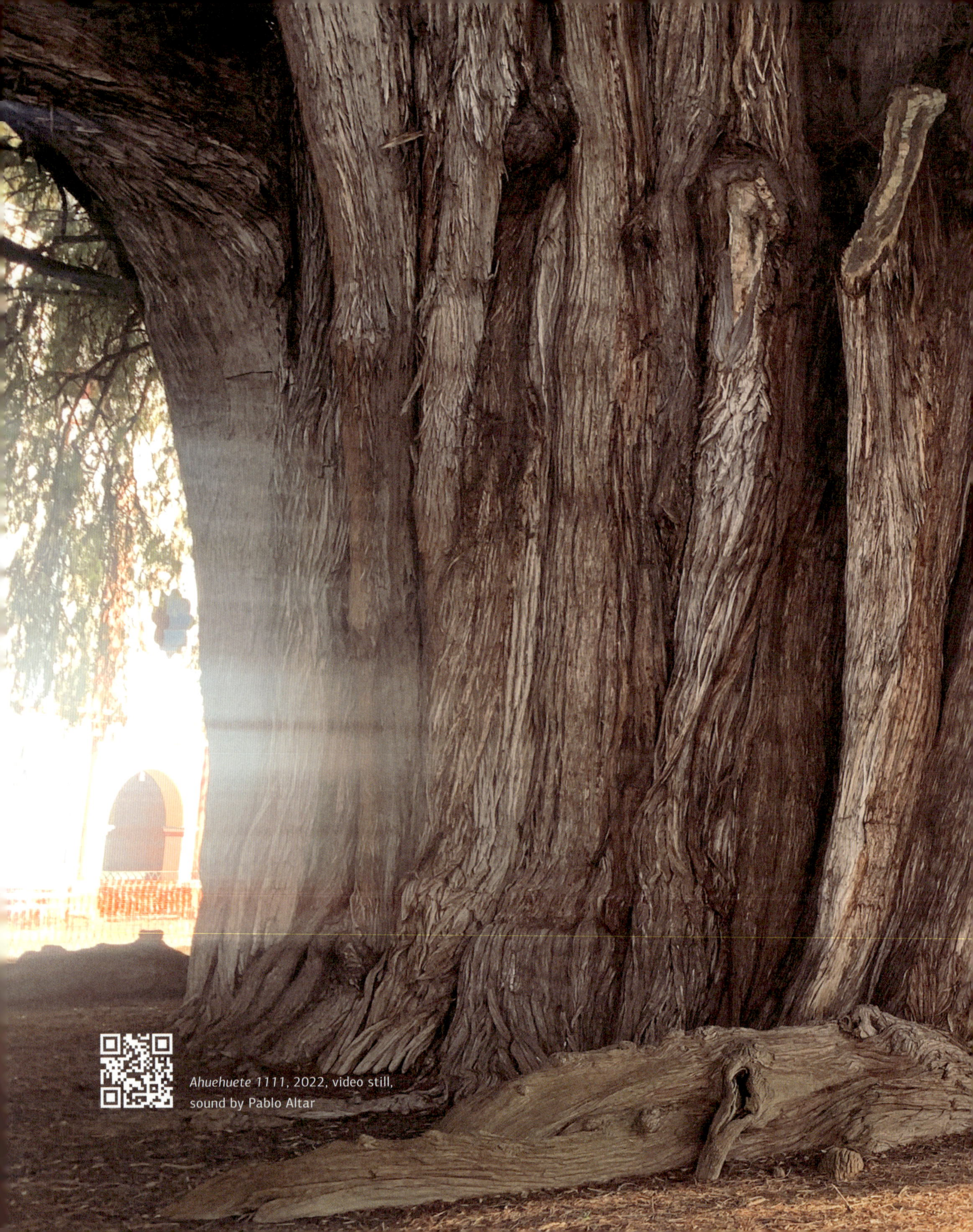

Ahuehuete 1111, 2022, video still,
sound by Pablo Altar

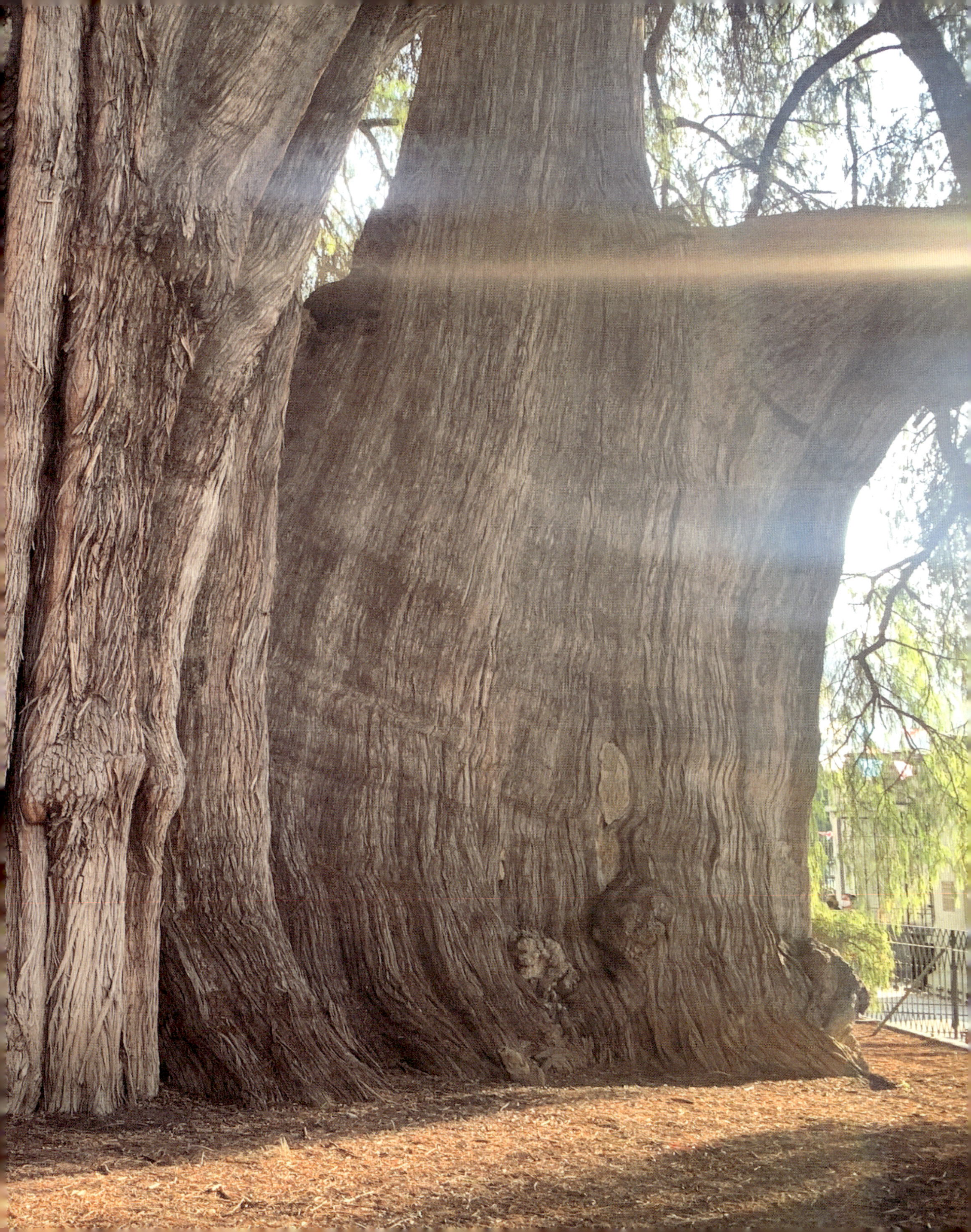

I don't want to say my name. I prefer to stay anonymous.
I can be everyone and nobody.
I can't describe myself. You know me already haha, yes, I'm those energy consuming thoughts. I can't feel the pain of your soul. I live for myself and only for myself.
I live for myself and only for myself. I'm satisfied when I'm right. I help you wear masks. I'm sure it 's the only way to protect you. I know it's also a way to feed your wounds. The more you ignore me, the more I exist in you. Of course I love to be complimented and to be recognized. I'll use every method to get more compliments hahaha hum hum hum Hum, I am a stranger who has lived in your soul for so long that you have forgotten about me. You have become homeless in your own home.
You feed me easily when someone hurts you. I'm so proud, not humble at all, I love comparing everything and judging everything. Hahahaha that's my funny game. Yes, I know (miamamiamaiamaiamaiamaia), the more you hate me, the more you think you will make me disappear. You think trying to destroy me is the solution but hahaha no baby. PERIOD.
I appreciate when you take care of me. That's when I truly exist.
I love to impose my values upon others, yes baby that's me, E G O E GO baby. I took this power indeed, a long time ago, long time ago. I don't remember exactly when Hehehe, I mean maybe when the fridge was created or the mirror or the concept of conscience or when Adam and Eve were banished from heaven. Or maybe when human beings discovered how to kill others.
I don't remember exactly when ... whatever ... but.
I can be destructive and you let me. I'm obsessive and not rational. I care about judgment from people.
(Yummy yummy) Emotional food.
E- G- O
I love finding justifications and who is responsible. Yes, that's me! I am always on the defensive hahaha annoying no?
E GO EGO EGO EGO I keep your traumas alive and help you to never forget them so that at the end of the day you are afraid to be another person.

Living in the past is my only way to exist.
Not fun, hum.
BAD BAD BAD GOOD GOOD, BAD BAD BAD GOOD GOOD GOOD OK
The more you feel guilty, the more living space you provide.
I imagine maybe one day I 'll open my heart and breathe and just just YES YES YES YES YES YES YES. What I mean is that you have to believe in self-love, release, release all the pain and fears I keep in my belly because I can't share it at all.
I know the way to calm me down, it's to love myself, accept myself with my all wrong details, with all my flaws. That 's the truth.
It's painful, I can't breathe. Instead of staying focused on LOVE LOVE LOVE. What is love?
(The song: What is love? Oh baby, don't hurt me, don't hurt me, no more)
(laughter) When you love someone you listen, I mean you try to understand, act and be present. no? No, so maybe I can hear myself because I'm already a part of yourself listen, welcome his fears and pains, maybe I can be more present for myself every day and stop being on the lookout everywhere.
I know I am this ugly belly and I have to accept myself and love myself, maybe I can accept others if I love myself.
I just want to control everything. That's it.
Not hearing my heart, only my brain and letting this brain-belly become bigger, bigger, bigger and bigger.
Why should I change? I'm power, I don 't care, those are my rules!
Yes, sure, sure. I don't feel comfortable deep inside of me, I think, but it's true, I'm weak and I'm ashamed to be weak. That's why. Weak is beautiful.
Weak is beautiful.
Hum hum that's why I don't want to say my name because I know they are going to shine a light on me that's why.
I don't want to say my name, I prefer to stay anonymous.

Soundfile

Obstacles move out of my way when I focus on the things that do me good, that bring me joy and are not detrimental to others.

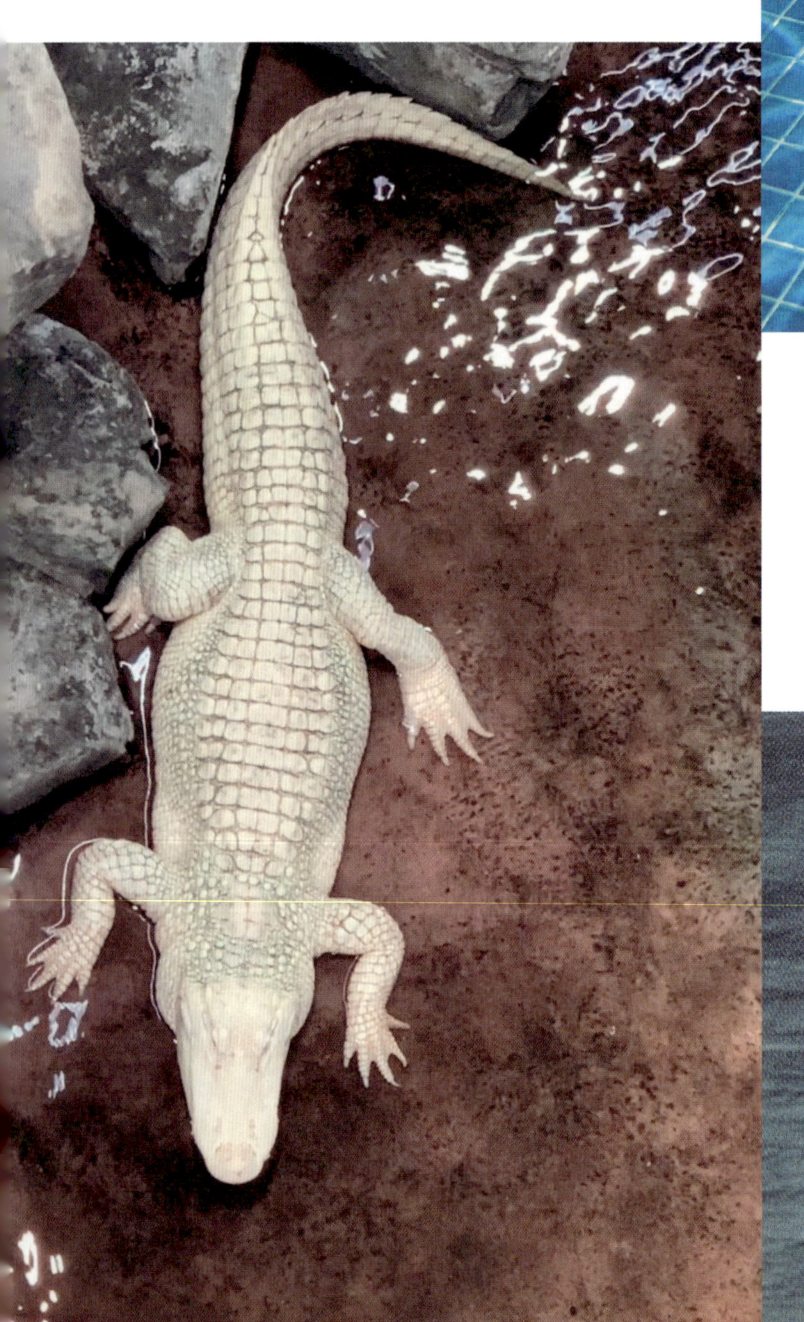

My life is only just beginning, post-Covid-19.

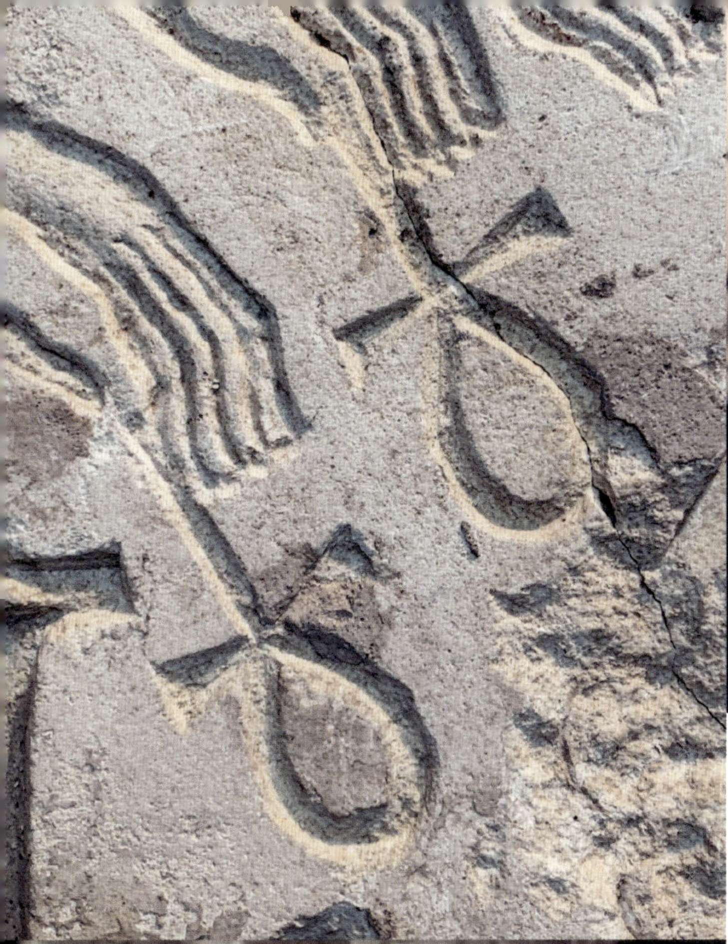

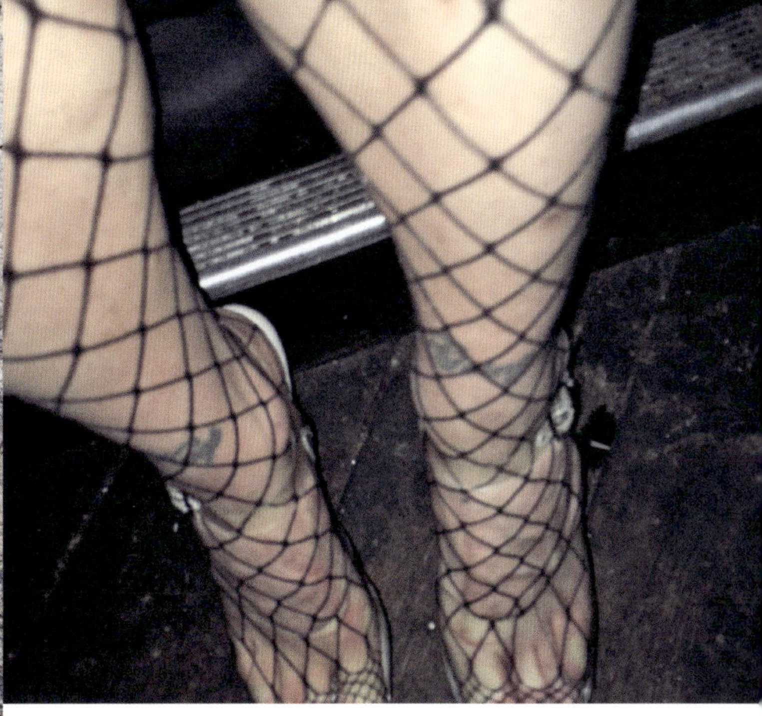

Love is political.
My body is political.

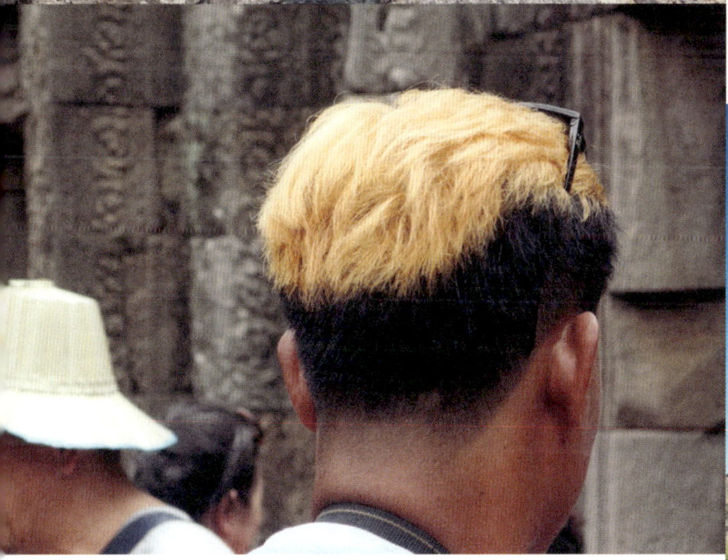

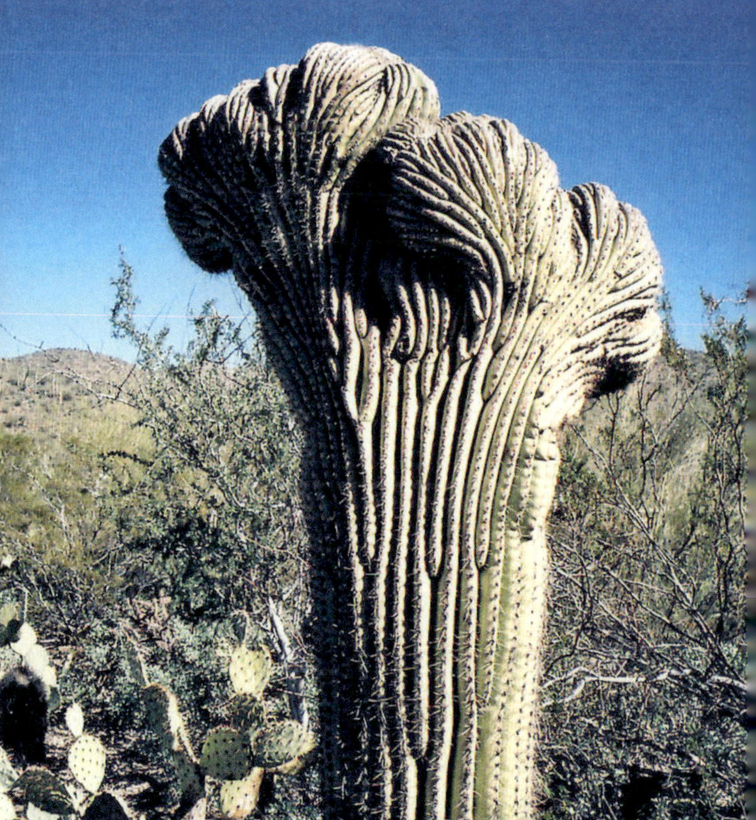

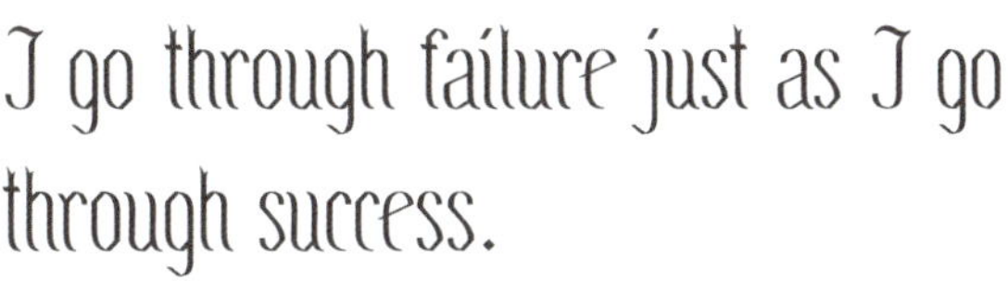

I go through failure just as I go through success.

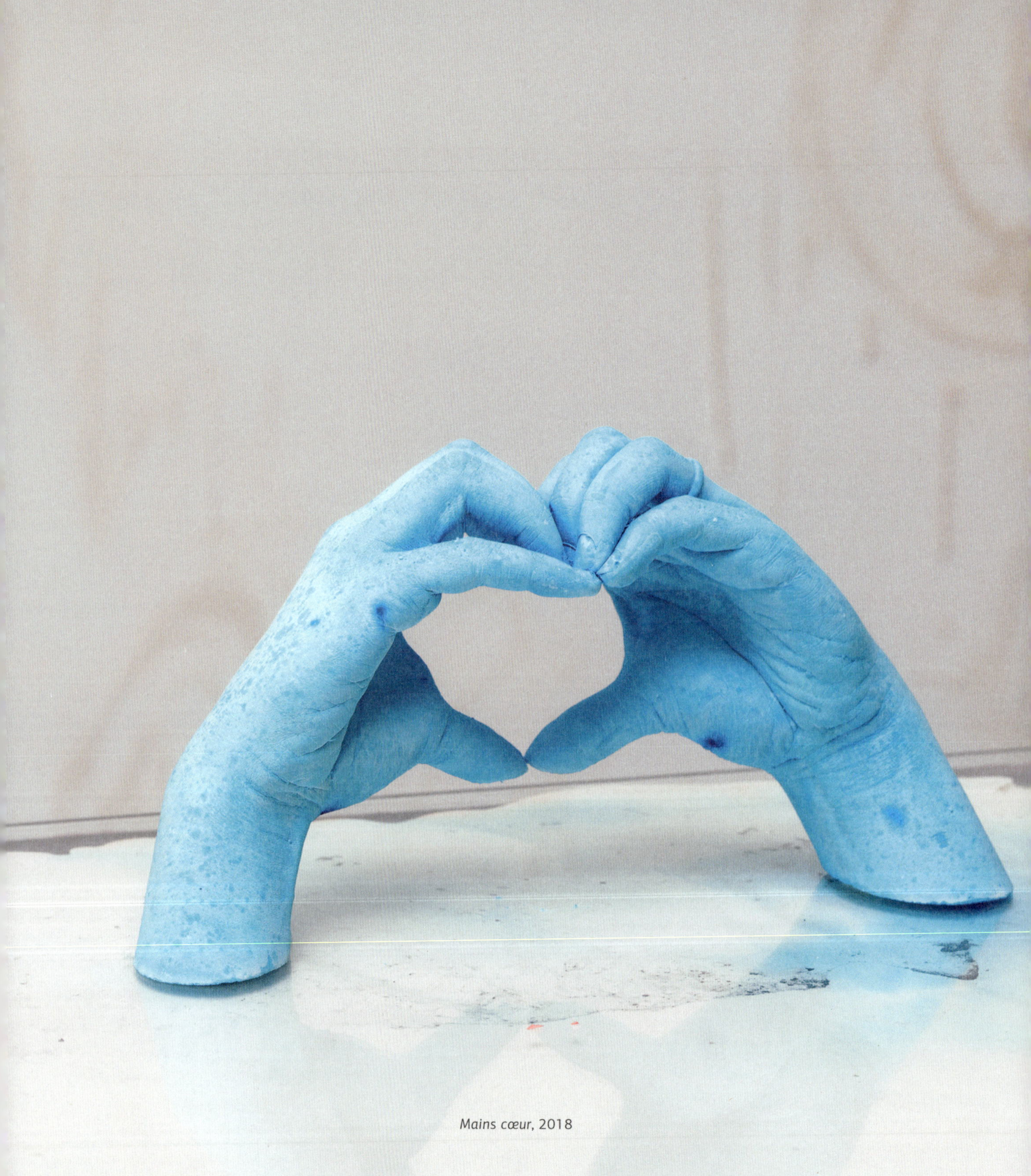

Mains cœur, 2018

Temple of Love

Temple of Love (Préface), 2018, Bétonsalon, Paris, France / Invitations: Hessie, Nadia Yala Kisukidi, Karim 555Kattan, Tarek Lakhrissi, KHNG KHAN and Ylvafalk, Cheapest University / Curator: Lucas Morin

Temple of Love – To be Engulfed, 2018, Zachęta Project Room, Warsaw, Poland / Invitations: Arghtee, Renata Hryciuk / Curator: Magda Kardasz

Temple of Love – Absence, 2019, MAC – Musée d'art contemporain de Lyon, France / Invitations: Ceel Mogami de Haas, Gaillard & Claude, Arghtee / Curators: Matthieu Lelièvre and Palais de Tokyo

Temple of Love – Adorable, 2019, The Mistake Room, Los Angeles, USA / Invitations: Carmen Brouard, Colburn School / Curator: Kris Kuramitsu

Temple of Love – Alteration, 2019, Curitiba Biennial, Oscar Niemeyer Museum, Brazil / Invitations: Um Baile Bom, Hélio Leites / Curators: Adolfo Montejo Navas and Tereza de Arruda

Temple of Love – Affirmation, 2020, MAM – Musée d'Art Moderne de Paris, Nuit Blanche, Paris, France / A project in collaboration with HOUSE OF NINJA

Temple of Love – Agony, 2020, Hamidrasha Gallery, Tel Aviv, Israel / Invitations: Madame Café, Megg Rayara Gomes de Oliveira, Anyes Noël, Audre Lorde, ASMRTheChew, Marie-Carmel Brouard, Crystallmess, Roxanne Maillet / Curator: Avi Lubin

Temple of Love – Attente, 2020, Gr_nd, Berlin, Germany Invitations: Asta Baradji, Issa N'Diaye, Hasan Mahmudul, Djeba Gandega, Assitan Zaoura, Ibrahima Konaté and Aissatou Diallo, Judith Balso, Julien Machillot and Victorine Grataloup for L'Ecole des Actes / Guests: Moritz Maria Karl, Sam Keogh, Marina Stanimirovic, Lukas Wegwerth

Temple of Love – Affirmation, 2021, Nuit Blanche Kyoto / ROHM Theatre Kyoto, Japan / The performance was realised in collaboration with Daiji Meguro (choreographer and dancer), Moe Matsuki, Sho Takiguchi and Ryonosuke Endo (dancers) / Co-organiser: ROHM Theatre Kyoto (Kyoto City Music, Arts and Culture Promotion Foundation) / Partner: Musée d'Art Moderne de Paris / Concept: Gaëlle Choisne / Stage direction (Kyoto version): Daiji Meguro / Performers: Ryonosuke Endo, Sho Takiguchi, Moe Matsuki, Daiji Meguro / Curator: Nadia Chalbi

Temple of Love – To be Ascetic (Tolalito), 2021, GIBCA: Göteborg International Biennial for Contemporary Art, Sweden / Curator: Lisa Rosendahl

Temple of Love – Love to Love, 2021, New Museum 2021 Triennial: Soft Water Hard Stone, New York, USA Curators: Margot Norton, Allen and Lola Goldring, Jamillah James

Temple of Love – Atopos, 2022, MAC VAL, Vitry-sur-Seine, France / Curators: MAC VAL and Gaëlle Choisne Invitations: Nge le, Aung Ko, Gloria Maso, Elisabetta Potasso, Roxanne Maillet, Célia Gaultier, Emanuelle Soum

Temple of Love – To Hide, 2022, Künstlerhaus Bethanien, Berlin, Germany / Invitations: Ahuehuete, Pablo Altar, Arghtee, ASMR STACY, Association Agonessan, Mykki Blanco, Marie-Carmel Brouard, Cardi B, Jean Chesnel, Crystallmess, Virgine Despentes, Sidney Drew, Léo Dupré, Silvia Federici, Nadia Yala Kisukidi, Zoe Leonard, Audre Lorde, Agnes Noel, Euvonie Reynald and Megg Rayara Gomes de Oliveira, Madame Café, Karl Marx, Nicki Minaj, Djibril Sall, Spice, Lorenzo Targhetta, Christiane Taubira, Simone Thiébaut, Assa Traoré, Françoise Vergès, Amber Wagner, Tierra Whack

List of Images

Pages 6–7, 32–33, 44–45, 54–55: Personal photographs belonging to Gaëlle Choisne, © the artist

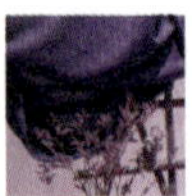

p. 10, 14 (right): *Paul Gilroy my bro*, 2022, sport tee printed in Mexico made in China, keys, chains, dry flowers , exhibition view of *Temple of Love – To Hide*, Künstlerhaus Bethanien, Berlin, Germany, 2022. Courtesy the artist, photo: David Brandt, © Künstlerhaus Bethanien

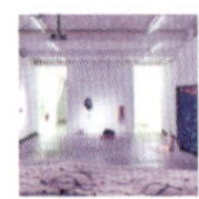 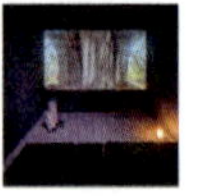 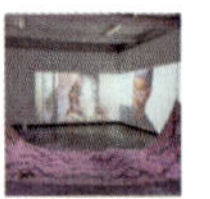 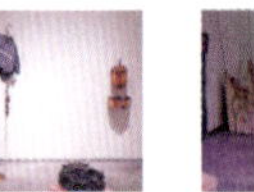 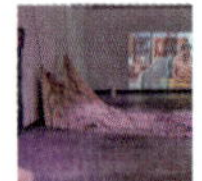

p. 11, 19–22, 24–25: ***Temple of Love – To Hide***, exhibition views, Künstlerhaus Bethanien, Berlin, Germany, 2022. Photo: David Brandt, © Künstlerhaus Bethanien

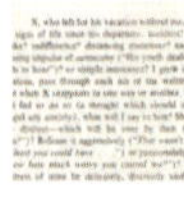

p. 13: Extract from the essay *A Lover's Discourse: Fragments* (1977) by Roland Barthes.

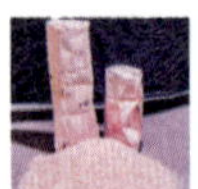 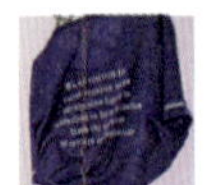

p. 14, left: ***My devotion for you*** (detail), 2022, candle with intentions, soya wax, natural pigments, dry flowers, ylang ylang, approx. 70x25x25 cm, exhibition view of *Temple of Love – To Hide*, 2022. Courtesy the artist, photo: David Brandt, © Künstlerhaus Bethanien

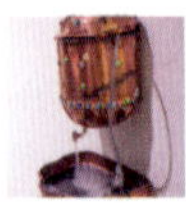

p. 15: ***Purple water-wishes and more foreva1111illimited love.)period.***, 2022, copper, flowers, pump, tattoos, gems, butterfly stickers, exhibition view of *Temple of Love – To Hide*, 2022. Courtesy the artist, photo: David Brandt, © Künstlerhaus Bethanien

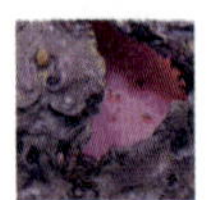

p. 16: ***L'éveil du cosmos*** (detail), 2022, olives, glazed ceramic, 60x50x40 cm. Courtesy the artist, photo: David Brandt, © Künstlerhaus Bethanien

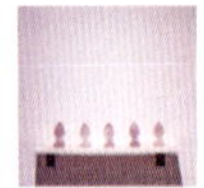 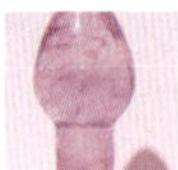 

p. 17, 23: ***Survival kit for straight ppl***, 2022, amethyst anal plug from China made by hand, wax and Himalayan salt shelf, exhibition views of *Temple of Love – To Hide*, Künstlerhaus Bethanien, Berlin, Germany, 2022. Courtesy the artist, photo: David Brandt, © Künstlerhaus Bethanien

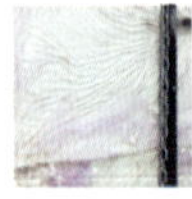 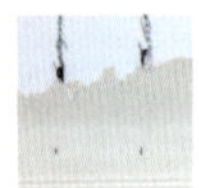 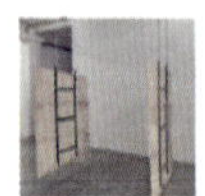 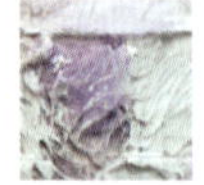

p. 18: ***Forget the appearances 5D***, 2022, empty screen, acrylic resin, fabric, measurements, exhibition view of *Temple of Love – To Hide*, 2022. Courtesy the artist, photo: David Brandt, © Künstlerhaus Bethanien

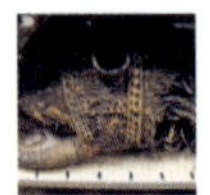 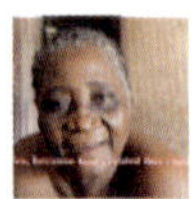 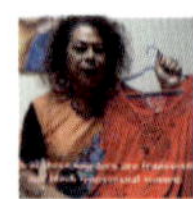

pp. 26, 28, 30: Stills from ***Accumulation Primitive***, 2019–2022, colour video, 16/9, 52 min 23 sec, © the artist

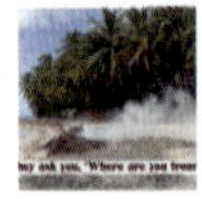 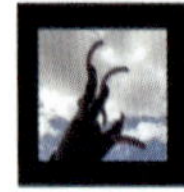

pp. 27, 29: Stills from ***Primitive Amnesia***, 2019–2022, colour video, 16/9, 52 min 23 sec, © the artist

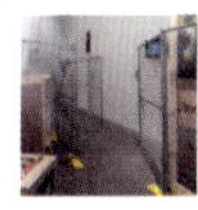

p. 35: ***Temple of Love – Love To Love***, installation view, *Triennial: Soft Water Hard Stone*, New Museum, New York, 2021. Photo: Dario Lasagni, © New Museum, New York and the artist

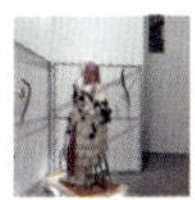

p. 36, left: ***Madone of gratefulness (make a wish and say thank you)***, 2021, plaster, ceramic, light, chains, dried flowers, metal threshold. Courtesy the artist, installation view of *Temple of Love – Love To Love*, photo: Dario Lasagni, © New Museum, New York and the artist

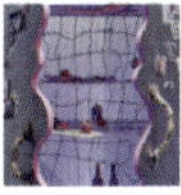

p. 36, right: ***Ego, he goes (Fridge selfspeech and shine love consciousness – Period!)***, 2021, metal, engraved acrylic glass, engraved and pigmented acrylic resin, sound system, engraved ceramic, photographs and found documents, magnets. Courtesy the artist, installation view of *Temple of Love – Love To Love*, photo: Dario Lasagni, © New Museum, New York and the artist

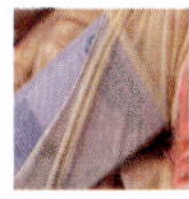

p. 38: ***Textus*** (detail), 2018–2022, textile, metal rings, list of books by the artist (3 books selected by the artists, the rest at the discretion of the purchaser)

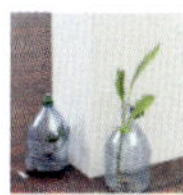

p. 39, left: ***Hors sol***, 2021–2022, plastic bottles, plant cuttings, protocol and video tutorial made by the artist with her mother

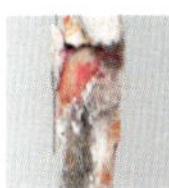

p. 39, right: ***Potomitan*** (detail), 2018, plaster, pigments, earth, gold-plated chain, all images exhibition views of *Temple of Love – Atopos*, MAC VAL – Musée d'Art Contemporain du Val-de-Marne, Vitry-sur-Seine, 2022. Production and courtesy MAC VAL musée d'art contemporain du Val-de-Marne and the artist, photo: Aurélien Mole

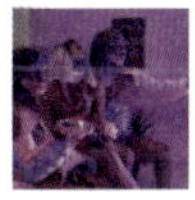 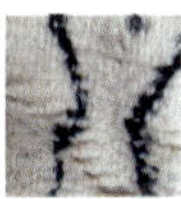

p. 40, 42: Performance ***Temple of Love – Affirmation***, 2020, project in collaboration with HOUSE OF NINJA, Nuit Blanche, Musée d'Art Moderne de la Ville de Paris, France. Courtesy MAM and the artist, photo: MAM

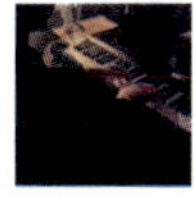

p. 46: ***Lie close to our ancestors*** (detail), 2020–2022, rug made by women at Association Agonessan in Ourika, Morocco, 7 x 2 m. Courtesy of Air de Paris, © the artist

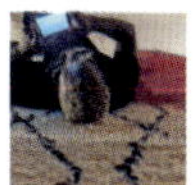 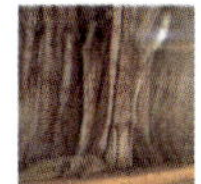

p. 47, 48: Portraits of Pablo Altar and Djibril Sall reading in the artist's studio prior to his performance for the opening of *Temple of Love – To Hide*, Künstlerhaus Bethanien, Berlin, Germany, 19 May 2022. Photo: the artist, © the artist

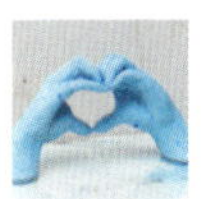

p. 50, 51: ***Ahuehuete 1111***, 2022, video still, © the artist

p. 56: ***Mains cœur***, 2018, glazed ceramic, acrylic resin tinted in the mass, silicone, dried flowers. Photo: Aurélien Mole

Biography

Gaëlle Choisne
Born in 1985 in Cherbourg, France
Lives and works in Berlin, Germany and Paris, France

SOLO EXHIBITIONS

2022 *Temple of Love – To Hide*, Künstlerhaus Bethanien, Berlin, Germany
Monument aux Vivant.e.s – CHOC, Palais de la Porte Dorée, Musée national de l'histoire de l'immigration, Paris, France
Temple of Love – Atopos, MAC VAL, Vitry-sur-Seine, France

2021 *Mondes Subtiles*, Air de Paris, Romainville, France
999, Gilles Drouault, galerie/multiples, Paris

2020 *DÉFIXION*, Musée archéologique Henri-Prades, Lattes, France
Temple of Love – Agony, Hamidrasha Gallery, Tel Aviv, Israel

2019 *Temple of Love – Adorable*, The Mistake Room, Los Angeles, USA
Temple of Love – To Be Engulfed, Zacheta Room Project, Warsaw, Poland

2018 *Temple of Love*, Bétonsalon, Paris
Hybris, Untilthen Gallery, Paris

2016 *Constellation hétéroclite*, Untilthen Gallery, Paris

2015 *C R I C C R A C*, La Centrale Galerie Powerhouse, Montreal, Canada
Cric Crac, Centre d'art contemporain – La Halle des bouchers, Vienne, France

SELECTED GROUP EXHIBITIONS

2022 *Dust Specks on the Sea*, Villa du Parc, Annemasse, France
Dust Specks on the Sea, La Ferme du Buisson, Noisiel, France
Des corps, des écritures, Musée d'Art moderne, Paris
Hypernuit, FRAC Nouvelle Aquitaine – MECA, Bordeaux, France
Separate/Together, Cooper Cole, Toronto, Canada

2021 *The situation is fluid*, Amsterdam Art Gallery, Rijksakademie, Amsterdam, Netherlands
Intérieurs 2020, curated by Musée d'art moderne de Paris, The National Museum of Modern Art, Kyoto, Japan
Dust Specks on the Sea: Contemporary Sculpture from the French Caribbean & Haiti, Little Haiti Cultural Center, Miami, USA; 516 ARTS, Albuquerque, New Mexico; San Francisco Art Institute, San Francisco, USA
Temple of Love – Atopos, GIBCA – Göteborg International Biennial for Contemporary Art, Gothenburg, Sweden
Temple of Love – Affirmation, Nuit Blanche, Kyoto, Japan
Soft Water Hard Stone, Temple of Love – Love to Love, 5th New Museum Triennial, New York, USA
Se souvenir du présent, esprits de l'assemblage, Le 19, Centre régional d'art contemporain, Montbéliard, France

	Femmes à l'oeuvre, organised by FRAC Nouvelle-Aquitaine MÉCA, Galerie d'art contemporain – LE MI[X], Mourenx, France
	Crystal Clear, Pera Museum, Istanbul, Turkey
2020	*Temple of Love – Affirmation*, in collaboration with HOUSE OF NINJA, Nuit Blanche, Musée d'Art Moderne de Paris, Paris
	Temple of Love – Attente, gr_und gallery, Berlin, Germany
	Even the rocks reach out to kiss you, Transpalette, Bourges, France
	Have you seen a horizon lately, MAACAL – Musée d'Art contemporain africain Al-Maaden, Marrakesh, Morocco
	Les moyens du bord, La Vilette x Centre Pompidou, Paris
	La vie des tables, Centre d'art contemporain d'Ivry – le Crédac, Ivry-sur-Seine, France
	La clinique du queer, Maison Populaire, Montreuil, France
2019	*Temple of Love – Absence*, MAC – Musée d'art contemporain, 15th Lyon Biennale, France
	Le Fil d'Alerte, 21ème Prix de la Fondation Ricard, Paris
	Fronteiras em Aberto, 14th Biennale de Curitiba, Musée Oscar Niemeyer, Curitiba, Brazil
	Aube immédiate, vents tièdes, Mécènes du sud, Montpellier, France
	Accumulation Primitive, Crédit Municipal de Paris, Paris
2018	*Plein jeu*, FRAC Champagne-Ardennes, Reims, France
	Inspiration – Transpiration, Maison des Arts et de la Culture de Créteil, Créteil, France
2017	*An unpredictable expression of human potential*, Sharjah Biennial 13, Beirut, Lebanon
	Rendez-vous, CAFA Art Museum, Beijing, China
2016	*Culture Pop Marauders*, Mains d'Oeuvres, Saint-Ouen, France
2015	*Rendez-Vous 15*, IAC – Institut d'art contemporain, 13th Lyon Biennale, Villeurbanne, France
	Lejos del Teclado, 12th Internationale Biennal of Havana, Havana, Cuba
	Cool as a state of mind, MAMO – Cité Radieuse, Marseille, France

RESIDENCIES AND AWARDS

2021–22	International Artist-in-Residence Programme of KfW Stiftung at Künstlerhaus Bethanien, Berlin, Germany
2021	Prix Aware, AWARE: Archives of Women Artists, Research and Exhibitions, guest curated by Thomas Conchou
2021	*À l'oeuvre*, residency and production support, Lafayette Anticipations, Paris, France
2019	Residency in Atelier Van Lieshout, Rotterdam, Netherlands
2017–18	Residency in Rijksakademie, Amsterdam, Netherlands
2016	*Traverses*, Villa Vassilieff, Residency Bétonsalon – Centre d'art et de recherche/ Cité internationale des arts, Paris, France

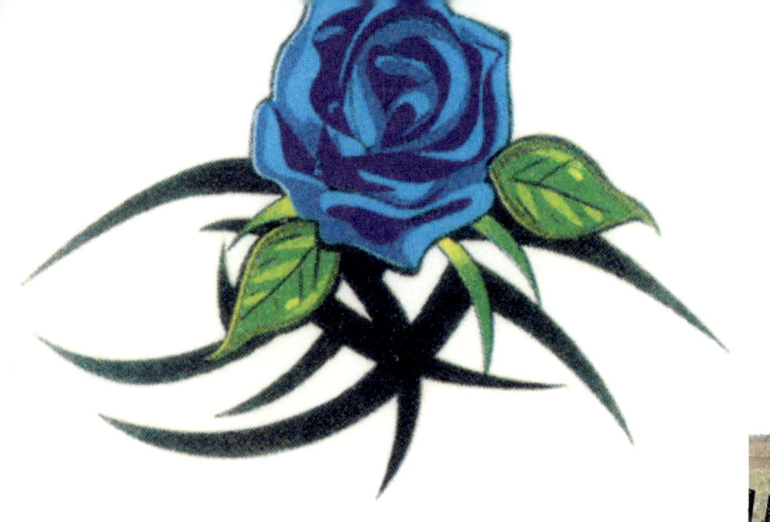

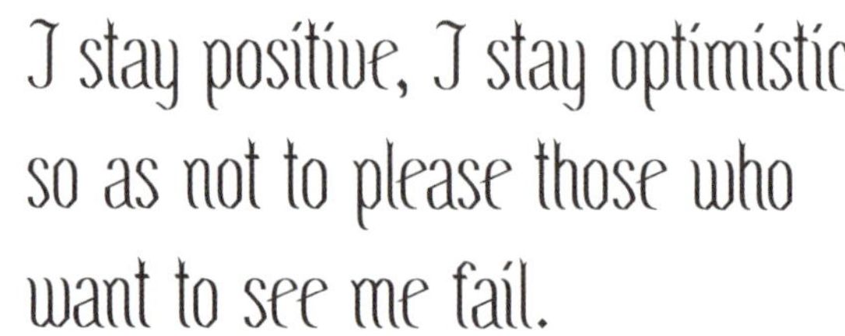

I stay positive, I stay optimistic so as not to please those who want to see me fail.

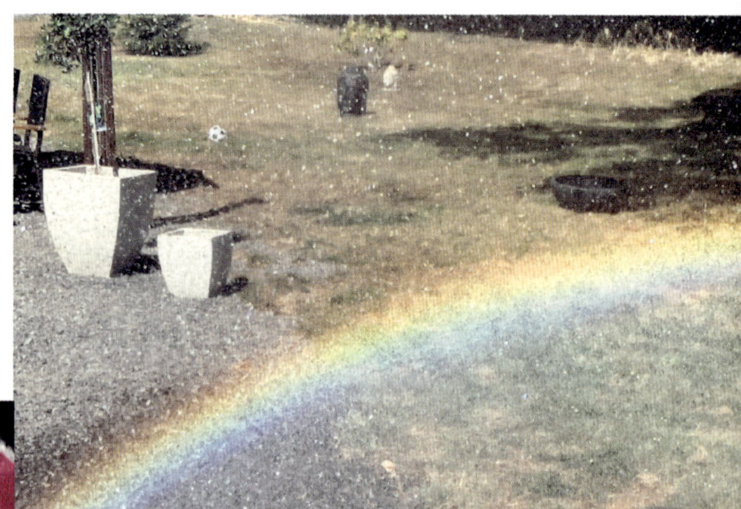

I love and respect myself unconditionally.

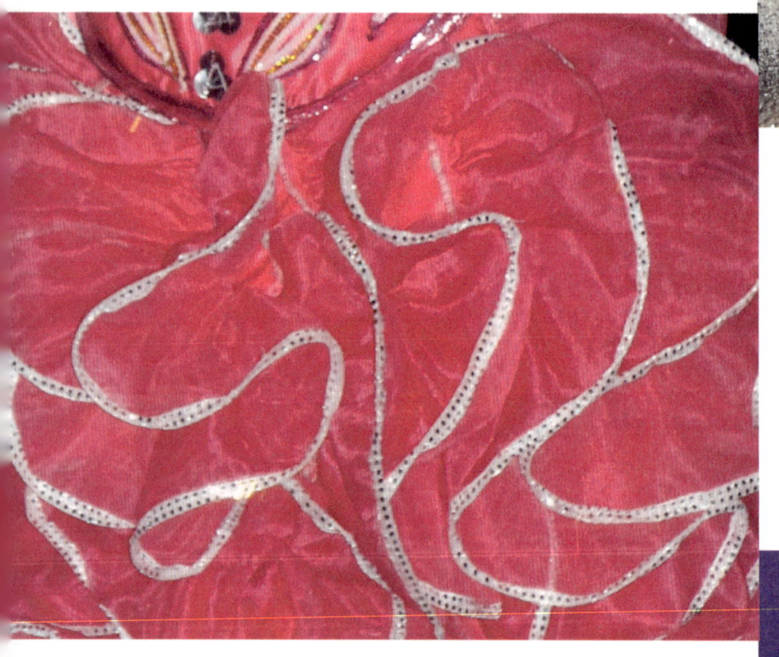

Knowing how to say no is to be free; for example, no to totalitarianism.

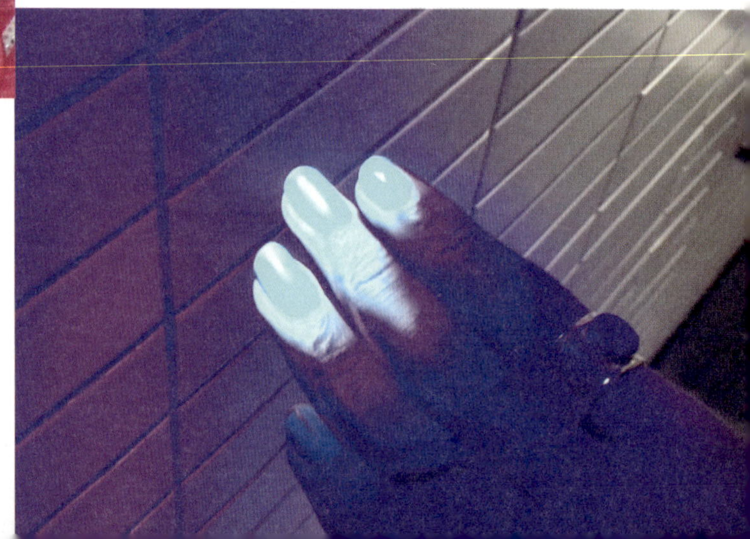

I respect others even if they don't respect me, because I respect myself.

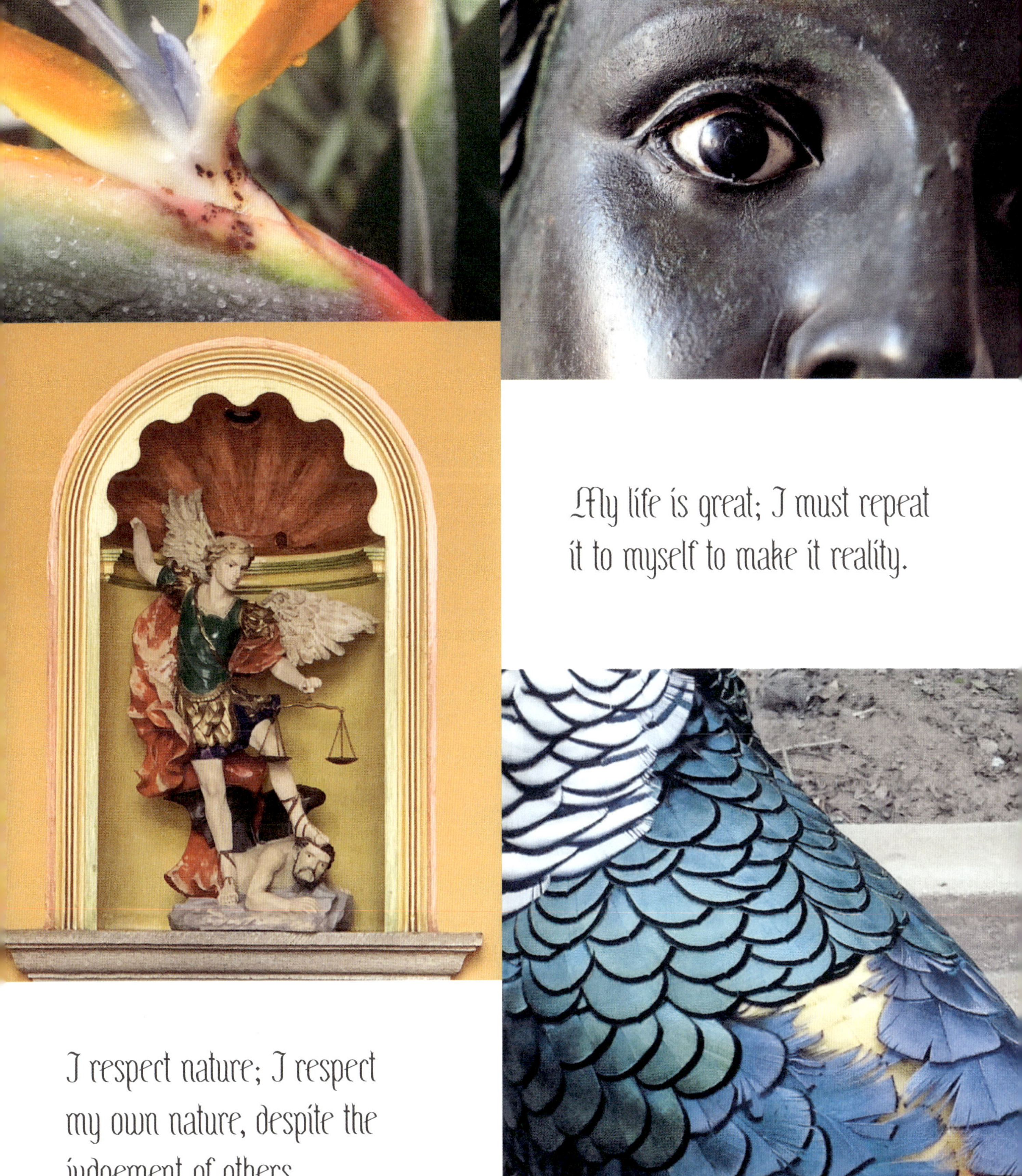

My life is great; I must repeat it to myself to make it reality.

I respect nature; I respect my own nature, despite the judgement of others.

Gaëlle Choisne – Temple of Love – To Hide
With an essay by Wong Binghao
Editors: Daniela Leykam, Christoph Tannert

Künstlerhaus Bethanien GmbH, Kohlfurter Straße 41/43, Showroom: Kottbusser Str. 10, D-10999 Berlin, www.bethanien.de
Artistic Director: Christoph Tannert / **Administrative Director:** Andrea Boche
International Studio Programme: Valeria Schulte-Fischedick / **Press & PR:** Maximilian Rauschenbach
Technical Staff: Peter Rosemann, Thomas Moll

KfW Stiftung, Palmengartenstraße 5–9, D-60325 Frankfurt am Main, www.kfw-stiftung.de
Managing Director: Michael Rösler / **Programme Manager Arts and Culture:** Daniela Leykam

Editing: Tomke Braun, Rose Field, Daniela Leykam / **Project Coordination:** Tomke Braun
Photos: Gaëlle Choisne, David Brandt, Dario Lasagni, Aurélien Mole
Translation: Dawn Gibbs, Nina Kettiger, Patrick Kremer / **Copy-editing:** Susannah Worth
Design: Thorsten Probst / angenehme-gestaltung.de / **Production:** Druckerei Kettler, Bönen

Published by Verlag Kettler, Dortmund, www.verlag-kettler.de

This catalogue is published on the occasion of the exhibition *Temple of Love – To Hide* by Gaëlle Choisne, International Studio Programme, Künstlerhaus Bethanien, Berlin, 19 May – 12 June 2022. Gaëlle Choisne is a grantholder of KfW Stiftung.

The artist would like to acknowledge the following institutions and people for their support: Wong Binghao, Tomke Braun, Thomas Conchou, Axelle Failleres, Rose Field, Memphis Krickeberg, KfW Stiftung, Künstlerhaus Bethanien, Lazlo, Daniela Leykam, Thorsten Probst, Djibril Sall, Valeria Schulte-Fischedick, Lorenzo Targhetta

Further publications of the book series so far: PARADISE / Thabiso Sekgala / January 2014, THE MADMAN SEES WHAT HE SEES / Carla Zaccagnini / March 2014, STORE IN A COOL AND DRY PLACE / Prajakta Potnis / November 2014, LIFE ON MARS / Stary Mwaba / March 2015, THE LAND BENEATH MY FEET / Khvay Samnang / September 2015, IN SILENCE / Nguyen Thi Thanh Mai / March 2016, INTENDING PROBABILITY / Salwa Aleryani / March 2017, AOS VENCEDORES AS BATATAS / Matheus Rocha Pitta / June 2017, EXIT – ENTRANCE / Orawan Arunrak / August 2017, ALL THAT IS SEEN AND UNSEEN / Vartan Avakian / January 2019 / FEEDING THE SCENE / Elia Nurvista / July 2019, RADIO CARABUCO / Andrés Pereira Paz / November 2019 / ... THESE GESTURES OF MEMORY / Gladys Kalichini / September 2020, MARBLE DUST / Talya Lubinsky / December 2020 / CULTURA PROFILÁCTICA / Hamlet Lavastida / May 2021, SCALES OF DECAY / Daniel Lie / October 2021

ISBN 978-3-98741-036-9 KÜNSTLERHAUS BETHANIEN 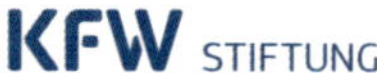